From Watt to the Great Exhibition

BRITAIN 1815–1851

Colin McNab
Robert Mackenzie

Oliver & Boyd

Oliver & Boyd
Robert Stevenson House
1–3 Baxter's Place
Leith Walk
Edinburgh EH1 3BB

A Division of Longman Group Ltd.

First published 1982
Third impression 1983

Selections and editorial matter
© Oliver & Boyd 1982

ISBN 0 05 003351 4

Printed in Singapore by
Tien Mah Litho Printing Co Pte Ltd

Introduction

We have written this book for students in the Third Year and upwards in the secondary school, studying Britain in the first half of the nineteenth century. It will be of direct use for the CSE and GCE O level topics on 'Britain, 1815–51' based on the Schools Council Project *History 13–16*. More specifically this text caters first and foremost for students studying the SCE O grade topic 'Britain from Waterloo to the Great Exhibition'.

The basis of the book is that of the contemporary sources used throughout. We hope these will be used to develop pupils' skills of interpretation and evaluation of historical evidence from the period, and to stimulate interest in doing so. However, our intention was not merely to provide a collection of historical source material; we set out to create a book suitable as a sole text for the study of the period 1815–51. Teachers who have further source materials of their own are of course free to add them as appropriate.

The questions and assignments coupled to the contemporary source extracts allow pupils in a mixed ability group to work at their own pace, under teacher guidance.

Contents

Acknowledgements

The authors and publishers wish to acknowledge permission given by Hamish Hamilton Ltd, London for the extracts from *The Great Hunger* by Cecil Woodham-Smith (© 1962, 1977 the Estate of Cecil Woodham-Smith) and by Lt. Cdr. John Hamilton of Rozelle for the extract from the Radical Address (*Rozelle Mss*).

They also wish to acknowledge permission given by the following for the use of illustrations on the pages shown: BBC Hulton Picture Library 10, 23, 38, 40, 41, 67 (left), 76, 78, 110, 167, 172, 173; Trustees of the British Museum 16, 26, 58; The Syndics of Cambridge University Library 174–5; The County Archivist, Cheshire Country Council 140; Durham County Library 102; Illustrated London News Picture Library 116; Mansell Collection 55, 69, 77, 97, 126, 134, 143, 157, 158, 159, 166, 176; Metropolitan Police Public Information Department 36; Trustees of the National Library of Scotland 67 (right), 79; Science Museum 146 (from a watercolour drawing by T P Rowlandson), 149, 151; County Archivist, Suffolk Record Office 88; Victoria & Albert Museum 171; Wellcome Institute for the History of Medicine 95 (by courtesy of the Wellcome Trustees).

Map and diagrams by Stephen Gibson.

1 Britain in 1815

Britain's Population

We can only estimate the size of Britain's population before 1801 from parish registers of births, marriages and deaths. These records were not usually very accurate, but we can calculate that in 1700, the population of England and Wales was about 5.5 million, and by 1750 it had risen to about 6.5 million. This was a steady increase, but after 1800 the population grew even faster.

Year	England and Wales	Scotland	Ireland	Total
1801	9.08 M	1.61 M	5.22 M	15.91 M
1811	10.30 M	1.85 M	5.96 M	18.11 M
1821	12.12 M	2.09 M	6.80 M	21.01 M

Why was Britain's population increasing so quickly?

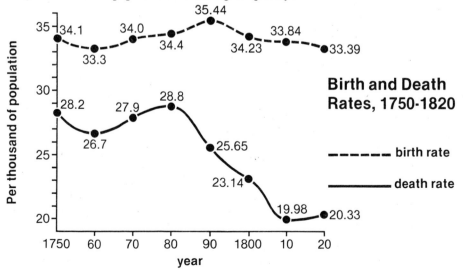

Birth and Death Rates, 1750-1820

- - - - - birth rate

———— death rate

Francis Place's explanation

... There are no such groups of half-starved, miserable, scald-headed children with rickety limbs and bandy legs as there were in the days of my youth, neither is there anything like the same mortality among them ...

Much of this is attributable to the increased salubrity of the Metropolis, much to the increase of surgical or medical knowledge, much also to the change that has taken place not only in London, but all over the country, in the habits of the working classes, who are infinitely more moral and more sober, more cleanly in their persons and their dwellings, than they were formerly, particularly the women, partly from the success of the cotton manufacture ... partly from an increased knowledge of domestic concerns and general management of children. Notwithstanding the vice, the misery and disease which still abounds in London, the general prevalence has been greatly diminished.

(Francis Place, *Principles of Population*, 1822)

The increase of surgical or medical knowledge mentioned by Place had not amounted to very much in the eighteenth century. Edward Jenner had discovered the process of vaccination which had helped to reduce the amount of smallpox, and this treatment was beginning to be applied to other diseases. However, outbreaks of disease were still very frequent. The number of hospitals had grown in the eighteenth century, but they were usually filthy places, and doctors at that time did not understand as much about disease and medicine as they do today.

To explain the rapid increase in Britain's population, we must look at the astonishing changes which were taking place at the time in both the countryside and the towns.

Changes in the Countryside

Until the eighteenth century, the land was still being farmed in much the same way as it had been for hundreds of years. The bulk of Britain's population lived in the southern half of England. Most people lived in country villages and earned their living by farming. They rented scattered strips of land from the local landowner, for growing crops such as oats, barley and wheat. They shared the common land on which all the villagers' animals grazed freely. This was the 'open-field' system, so called because each tenant's strips of land were not separated from neighbouring strips, nor from the common grazing land, by any fences or hedges. It worked fairly well until Britain's population began to increase in the eighteenth century. With more mouths to feed, the old system could not cope, and farmers began to look for more efficient ways of producing food.

Farming improvements

Landowners introduced all sorts of improvements. Lord Townshend in Norfolk was a leading figure in the 'Agrarian Revolution', using methods he had seen while Britain's ambassador in Holland.

> As I shall presently leave Norfolk it will not be improper to give a slight review of the husbandary which has rendered the name of this county so famous in the farming world . . . The great improvements have been made by means of the following circumstances:
> First. By inclosing without the assistance of Parliament.
> Second. By a spirited use of marl and clay.
> Third. By the introduction of an excellent course of crops.
> Fourth. By the culture of turnips well hand-hoed.
> Fifth. By the culture of clover and ray-grass.
> Sixth. By landlords granting long leases.
> Seventh. By the country [county] being divided chiefly into large farms.
> . . . still the whole success of the undertaking depends on this point: no fortune will be made in Norfolk by farming unless a judicious rotation of crops be pursued. That which has been chiefly adopted by the Norfolk farmers is:
> 1. Turnips; 2. Barley; 3. Clover; or clover and ray-grass; 4. Wheat.
> . . . This is a noble system, which keeps the soil rich; one exhausting crop is followed by a cleansing [one].
> . . . no small farmer would effect such great things as have been done in Norfolk. Inclosing, marling . . . belong absolutely and exclusively to great farmers . . . Great farms have been the soul of Norfolk culture: split them into tenures of a hundred pounds a year, you will find nothing but beggars and weeds in the whole county.
> (Arthur Young, *The Farmer's Tour through the East of England*, 1771)

'Inclosing' (or more commonly 'enclosing') meant doing away with the open-field system of scattered strips and common land. In its place appeared large fields with fences, hedges and ditches. On these 'enclosures' the farmers could use the new methods described by Arthur Young. Animals could now be separated from crops, and from one another. Men such as Robert Bakewell from Leicestershire began proper stock-breeding to produce distinct breeds of animals which were much larger and heavier than before.

The 'Improvers' in Scotland copied the farming improvements in England with great success.

> East Lothian led the way in Scotland to the improvement of husbandry, of enclosing, and of artificial grasses . . .
>
> The late John Cockburn of Ormiston was indefatigable in giving an example of good husbandry, by promoting it in his own estate. He conversed familiarly with his tenants; he gave them the best instructions; and patronised those greatly who co-operated with him in his various improvements.
>
> Robert Wight, one of his tenants on a farm of several hundred acres, gave an example to the rest. He enclosed his whole farm with hedge and ditch, and planted trees, all at his own expense.
>
> (A. Wight, *The Present State of Husbandry in Scotland, 1774–84*, vol. II 1778, pp. 131–4)

All these farming improvements meant more food of better quality than before, and a more varied diet. Since people were better-fed and healthier, the death-rate fell, and Britain's population increased.

QUESTIONS

1 *Calculate how much the population increased on average each year:*
   (a) In England and Wales from 1700 to 1750.
   (b) In England and Wales from 1750 to 1801.
   (c) In the whole of Britain from 1801 to 1820.
   What difference do you notice?
2 *What happened to the (i) birth rate, and (ii) death rate in Britain between 1780 and 1820? List the reasons Francis Place gives for these changes.*
3 *(a) Which new crops did Norfolk farmers begin to use?*
   (b) Why does Arthur Young say that a root crop (such as turnips) or clover should follow a grain crop (such as barley or wheat)?
   (c) How does he suggest the soil be fertilised?
   (d) What advantages did enclosures have over the open-field system for farmers?
   (e) Look at the improvements made by Robert Wight in East Lothian. Why

would such a tenant farmer want a 'long lease' as advised by Arthur Young?
4   How did these farming improvements help to increase Britain's population?

The effects of enclosures

At first, local landowners had to get Parliament to pass a special Enclosure Act so that they could go ahead and enclose the land of a village. This meant that thousands of Enclosure Acts were passed in the second half of the eighteenth century. To make matters simpler, Parliament passed a General Enclosure Act in 1801. This said that village land could be enclosed provided that the owners of most of the land agreed. This meant that the objections of small landowners and tenant-farmers could be ignored. Now, more land than ever was enclosed.

Landowners needed to enclose their land so that they could introduce the new methods in farming. However, enclosures usually meant larger farms and much higher rents than before. Many tenant-farmers found it impossible to pay such rents, with serious results:

> 1. The land-owner . . . unites several small farms into one, raises rent to the utmost . . . Thus thousands of families, which formerly gained an independent livelihood on those separate farms, have been gradually reduced to the class of day-labourers. But day-labourers are sometimes in want of work, and are sometimes unable to work; and in either case they resort to the parish. It is a fact, that thousands of parishes have not now half the number of farmers which they had formerly. And in proportion as the number of farming families has decreased, the number of poor families has increased.
> (The Rev. D. Davies, *The Case of the Labourers in Husbandry*, 1795, pp. 55–57)

> Its present occupant has within a few years managed to dispossess seven or eight dependent cottagers . . . These, being turned adrift found no other resource at least for their children, than that of sending them to the great manufactories.
> Elvanfoot, Clydesdale.
> (I. Lettice, *Letters on a Tour Through Scotland in 1792*)

The people who benefited from enclosure and other farming improvements were those landowners who could afford them and those tenant-farmers who could afford the increased rents which landowners now asked.

Those who could not afford to pay for improving their land, and tenants who could not pay the higher rents, were faced with a difficult choice. Some of them left the countryside altogether and looked for work in the towns. Some tenant-farmers who stayed had to give up the land they rented, and find work as landless farm labourers. This was perhaps the worst-paid job of all, and rising prices in the early nineteenth century made matters worse for these unfortunate labourers. Also, fewer people were required to work the land, so many labourers were unemployed for long periods.

William Cobbett, who championed the old system of farming, travelled the countryside observing the changes in country life:

> In all the really agricultural villages and parts of the kingdom, there is a *shocking decay*; a great dilapidation and constant pulling down or falling down of houses. The farm houses are not so many as they were forty years ago by three fourths. That is to say ... the infernal system ... has annihilated three parts out of four of the farm houses. The labourers' houses disappear also ... These enclosures ... are a *waste*; ... they are a proof of national decline and not of prosperity ... all manner of schemes have been resorted to get rid of the necessity of *hands*; ...
> (William Cobbett, *Rural Rides*, p. 67)

The Speenhamland system

In 1795, the magistrates in the parish of Speenhamland in Berkshire thought they had found a solution to the problem of the poverty of landless labourers. They began a scheme by which labourers in need received a weekly payment based on the cost of living. This 'Speenhamland system' was widely copied in other parishes throughout the agricultural south of England. Instead of solving the problem, however, it actually made matters worse.

> Resolved unanimously,
> That the present state of the Poor does require further assistance than has been generally given them.
> Resolved,
> ... that they [that is, the magistrates] will ... make the following calculations and allowances for the relief of all poor and industrious men and their families, who to the satisfaction of the Justices of their Parish, shall endeavour (as far as they can) for their own support and maintenance.
> That is to say,
> *When the Gallon Loaf of Second Flour, weighing 8 lb. 11 ozs. [almost 4 kg] shall cost 1s [5p].*

Then every poor and industrious man shall have for his own support 3s. weekly, either produced by his own or his family's labour, or an allowance from the poor rates, and for the support of his wife and every other of his family, 1s.6d.

When the Gallon Loaf shall cost 1s. 4d.

Then every poor and industrious man shall have 4s. weekly for his own, and 1s. and 10d. for every other of his family.

And so on in proportion, as the price of bread rise or falls (that is to say) 3d. to the man, and 1d. to every other of the family, on every 1d. which the loaf rise above 1s.

By order of the Meeting,
W. BUDD, Deputy Clerk of the Peace.

(The *Reading Mercury*, 11 May 1795)

This is part of a table published by the Speenhamland magistrates.

	Income should be for a Man	For a Single Woman	For a Man and his Wife	With one Child	With two Children
When the gallon loaf is 1s.0d.[5p]	3s.0d.[15p]	2s.0d.[10p]	4s.6d.[22½p]	6s.0d.[30p]	7s.6d.[37½p]
When ″ ″ 1s.1d.	3s.3d.	2s.1d.	4s.10d.	6s.5d.	8s.0d.
When ″ ″ 1s.2d.	3s.6d.	2s.2d.	5s.2d.	6s.10d.	8s.6d.
When ″ ″ 1s.3d.	3s.9d.	2s.3d.	5s.6d.	7s.3d.	9s.0d.
When ″ ″ 1s.4d.	4s.0d.	2s.4d.	5s.10d.	7s.8d.	9s.6d.

Here is part of an interview with Thomas Pearce, a Sussex labourer, in 1834. It clearly shows the effect of the Speenhamland system of poor relief on the labourers' attitude to work.

'In your parish are there many able-bodied men upon the parish?'

'There are a great many men in our parish who like it better than being at work.'

'Why do they like it better?'

'They get the same money and don't do half so much work. They don't work like me; they be'ant at it so many hours, and they don't do so much work when they be at it; they're doing no good, and are only waiting for dinner time and night; they be'ant working, it's only waiting.'

'How have you managed to live without parish relief?'
'By working hard.'
'What do the paupers say to you?'
'They blame me for what I do. They say to me "What are you working for?" I say "For myself!" They say "You are only doing it to save the parish, and if you didn't do it, you would get the same as another man has, and would get the money for smoking your pipe and doing nothing." 'Tis a hard thing for a man like me.'
(*Report of the Poor Law Commission*, 1834)

Many farmers unfairly lowered their labourers' wages. They knew that the labourers would receive enough money from the parish poor rate to buy bread for themselves and their families.

QUESTIONS

1   *Why did landowners charge higher rents for the enclosed farms they created?*
2   *Imagine you were a tenant-farmer who was unable to pay the increased rent your landlord was demanding. Write a paragraph outlining the choices facing you in deciding your future. How might you feel about your future?*
3   *As more and more land was enclosed, what happened to:*
     (a) The number of people living on the land?
     (b) the condition of many country villages?
4   *(a) What two things determined the amount of money an unemployed (or low-paid) labourer received on the Speenhamland scale?*
     (b) Why did the Speenhamland system have a bad effect on labourers who were in work?
     (c) Show how the Speenhamland system kept down the level of labourers' wages.

Changes in Industry

Domestic industry

As we have seen, before 1815 most people in Britain lived in the countryside and farmed for a living. They also produced cloth – either linen, wool or cotton – in their own homes. The raw materials were brought to them by merchants, and the villagers would spin it into thread, and then weave the thread into cloth, using their own spinning wheel and hand-loom in their own cottages. The merchants returned to collect the finished cloth and pay the villagers for their work.

> ... The distaff, the spinning wheel ... and subsequently the mule and jenny, were to be found forming part of the complement of household furniture ... whilst the cottage everywhere resounded with the clack of the hand-loom.
>
> These were, undoubtedly, the golden times of manufacture ... he [the artisan] generally earned wages which were sufficient not only to live comfortably upon, but which enabled him to rent a few acres of land ... It cannot, indeed, be denied, that his farming was too often slovenly ... and that the land yielded but a small proportion of what, under a better system of culture, it was capable of producing. It nevertheless ... gave him employment of a healthy nature, and raised him a step in the scale of society above the mere labourer.
>
> ... the small farmer, spinner, or hand-loom weaver, presents as orderly and respectable an appearance as could be wished. It is true that the amount of labour gone through, was but small; that the quantity of yarn or cloth produced was but limited – for he worked by the rule of his strength and convenience. They were, however, sufficient to clothe and feed himself and family decently ... to lay by a penny for an evil day ... and to enjoy those amusements ... then in being. He was a respectable member of society; a good father, a good husband, and a good son.
>
> (Peter Gaskell, *The Manufacturing Population of England: Its Moral, Social and Physical Conditions, and the Changes which have arisen from the Use of Steam Machinery*, 1833, Chapter 1)

The new inventions

From about the middle of the eighteenth century, new types of machinery began to be invented, first for spinning, then for weaving. These machines were soon to mean the end of domestic industry. In 1764 James Hargreaves, a Blackburn man, invented the 'Spinning Jenny', which could spin up to 80 threads at a time instead of one. It could be powered by hand, and it was still small enough to fit into a cottage. The first invention which could not be used in the home was Richard Arkwright's 'Water-frame.'

> ... he invented, about the year 1768, his present method of spinning cotton ... He soon made his machine practicable, and in 1769 he took out a

patent . . . He and his partners erected a mill at Nottingham, which was driven by horses; but this mode of turning the machinery being found too expensive, they built another mill on a much larger scale at Cromford, in Derbyshire, which was turned by a water-wheel, and from this circumstance the spinning machine was called the *water-frame* . . .

The factory system in England takes its rise from this period. Hitherto the cotton manufacture had been carried on almost entirely in the houses of the workmen . . . the spinning-wheel, and the loom, required no larger apartment than that of a cottage . . . But the water-frame . . . required more space than could be found in a cottage, and more power than could be applied by the human arm. Their weight also rendered it necessary to place them in strongly-built mills, and they could not be advantageously turned by any power then known but that of water . . . .

(Sir Edward Baines, *History of the Cotton Manufacture in Great Britain*, 1835, pp. 148–53, 182–5, 193–5)

Arkwright's machine was larger, more powerful and faster than a 'Spinning Jenny'. In 1779, Samuel Crompton's 'Mule' speeded up the process of spinning even more. It could be powered by steam, and made a stronger and finer thread than the water-frame. The 'Mule', used in large factories, put an end to spinning in the home. Weaving was still done on the hand-loom, but that too was to be brought to an end.

A Scot, James Watt, (see Chapter 5, page 79) developed a steam engine in 1769 which was an improvement on an earlier engine by Thomas Newcomen, and in 1781 Watt's engine was adapted so that it could drive a wide variety of factory machinery. Then in 1785 Edmund Cartwright invented a power loom which meant that weaving as well as spinning could be done in factories.

Crank Mill, Morley, Yorkshire. Built in 1790 it was one of the first steam driven mills.

By 1815, almost all of Britain's cloth was being produced in factories in the new industrial towns. It was now made much faster and in far greater quantities than before. Because of the growth of the textile industry, other industries also developed quickly. More iron was needed for machinery, and great ironworks were established, using Britain's natural supplies of iron ore. The first of these was the Carron Works near Falkirk, founded in 1759. 'Iron Masters', such as John Wilkinson in the English Midlands and the Crawshays in South Wales, made fortunes out of the demand for iron. Also, far more coal was needed to provide steam power for the new factories, and for smelting iron ore in the ironworks.

The Movement of Population

Robert Owen, the enlightened factory owner at New Lanark (see Chapter 5) reported on the changes in employment which had taken place up to 1815:

> Those who were engaged in the trade, manufactures, and commerce of this country thirty or forty years ago formed but a very insignificant portion of the knowledge, wealth, influence, or population of the Empire.
>
> Prior to that period, Britain was essentially agricultural. But, from that time to the present, the home and foreign trade have increased in a manner so rapid and extraordinary as to have raised commerce to an importance, which it never previously attained in any country possessing so much political power and influence.
>
> (By the returns to the Population Act in 1811, it appears that in England, Scotland and Wales there are 895 998 families chiefly employed in agriculture – 1 129 049 families chiefly employed in trade and manufactures – 640 500 individuals in the army and navy – and 519 168 families not engaged in any of these employments. It follows that nearly half as many more persons are engaged in trade as in agriculture – and that of the whole population the agriculturists are about 1 to 3.)
>
> This change has been owing chiefly to the mechanical inventions which introduced the cotton trade into this country, and to the cultivation of the cotton tree in America ... this trade created ... an extraordinary demand ... for human labour.
> (Robert Owen, 'Observations on the Effect of the Manufacturing System', 1815)

More and more people, therefore, were moving from the countryside to find work in the new factory towns and cities. These lay on or near the coalfields which provided the power for the 'Mules' and power looms of the factories. In Scotland, these towns were in the Central Lowlands, especially in the Clydeside area around Glasgow. In England, they were concentrated in Lancashire, South Yorkshire, Tyneside, Nottinghamshire, Derbyshire and in the 'Black Country' around Birmingham. In Wales, the area of greatest population growth was the south.

QUESTIONS

1 (a) What machines were used in the manufacture of cloth in the domestic system? How were they powered?
   (b) What was Peter Gaskell's opinion of the way of life he describes in the passage? List its advantages and disadvantages, according to the writer.
2 (a) Why could the 'Water-frame', the 'Mule' and the power loom not be used in the cottages of the workers, as earlier machines could?
   (b) Why did the growth of the iron and coal industries follow the change from domestic to factory manufacture of cloth?
3 (a) Look at the extract by Robert Owen. Ignoring the number of unemployed families, and the number of men in the army and navy, work out: (i) the proportion of the population working in agriculture; (ii) the proportion of the population working in trade and industry.
   (b) What reason does Robert Owen give for the increase in the number of people working in factories?
   (c) In which parts of Britain did most people live: (i) in the early eighteenth century, before the 'Industrial Revolution'? (ii) by 1815?

ASSIGNMENTS

A. Set out the arguments for and against the introduction of the new methods of farming in the eighteenth and early nineteenth centuries.
B. Construct a conversation which might have taken place between a worker in domestic industry and the owner of a new textile factory. Each person is arguing for his or her own method of working.

2 Unrest after 1815

By 1815, Britain had been at war with France almost continuously for 22 years. The long period of war ended with the Duke of Wellington's victory over Napoleon at Waterloo in 1815, but peace did not bring the expected prosperity and contentment.

Reasons for Widespread Discontent

Workers in town and country

We have already seen in Chapter 1 how enclosures and other changes in farming methods caused distress in the countryside amongst landless labourers. Their wages were kept down by the Speenhamland system (although this was not intended) in many parts of Britain. In the expanding industrial towns, most factory workers were forced to work in dreadful conditions for very low wages (See Chapter 5, page 64). Many of them had recently left the countryside to escape the distress there. Trade Unions might have helped to bargain for better working conditions, but such organisations had been made illegal by the Combination Acts 1799–1800. Henry Hobhouse, the Under-Secretary of State for the Home Department, explained the government's reasons for banning trade unions in a letter to the Rev W.R. Hay, Manchester:

> *14 August 1818*
> .... Matters have certainly been better managed at Stockport than at Manchester. The masters have been more firm, and the convictions under the Combination Act have done great service . . . the first object is to show to the workmen that the law is strong enough, if it be but properly enforced . . .
> (Home Office 79/3/195–7; quoted in A. Aspinall, *The Early English Trade Unions*)

In a letter to Major-General Sir John Byng, Hobhouse emphasised that Lord Liverpool's Tory Government was determined to enforce these laws strictly.

30 July 1818
. . . Even if the views of the unemployed workmen were originally unmixed
with politics, it is too much to expect that they should remain so, when they
are daily and nightly exposed to the harangues of such men as Drummond,
Bagguley etc. [These were well-known working class agitators of the time.]
It would therefore be an important measure if the magistrates could find
sufficient ground for taking those [men] into custody . . .
(Home Office, 79/3/239–40, in A. Aspinall, *The Early English Trade
Unions*)

The hand-loom weavers

Years before, when factories only spun thread, the hand-loom weavers were in
great demand, and earned a very good living:

> . . . Four days did the weaver work, for then four days was a week . . . and
> such a week to a skilled workman brought forty shillings. Sunday, Monday
> and Tuesday were of course jubilee. Lawn frills gorged freely from under
> the wrists of his fine blue, gilt-buttoned coat. He dusted his head with white
> flour on Sunday, smirked, and wore a cane. Walked in clean slippers on
> Monday. Tuesday heard him talk war bravado . . . and get drunk. Weaving
> commenced gradually on Wednesday . . .
> (William Thom, *Rhymes and Recollections of a Handloom Weaver*, London,
> 1845, p. 9)

But trade was reduced during the wars against France, and when more and
more factories began to use power looms (see Chapter 1, page 10), there was less
and less work for the hand-loom weavers, who rapidly went out of business.

> A very good hand-loom weaver will weave two pieces of cloth, each 24
> yards long. A steam loom weaver . . . will in the same time weave 7 similar
> pieces . . . the work done in the steam factory containing 200 looms would,
> if done by handloom weavers, find employment and support for a popula-
> tion of more than 2000 persons.
> (Richard Guest, *A Compendious History of the Cotton Manufacture*, 1823)

The Luddites

Other workers, too, feared that the new machinery would put them out of work. In
some cases, they took their revenge on the machines which they saw as the cause

of the trouble. These 'Luddites' (so called because they were supposed to be organised by a Ned Ludd) began machine-breaking in Nottinghamshire in 1811. They attacked 'wide-frames' used in stocking manufacture because these frames caused unemployment and also produced poor quality goods. 'Luddite' riots spread to Lancashire, Cheshire and Yorkshire. In some cases, factory owners were given a warning:

> SIR,
>
> Information has just been given in, that you are a holder of these detestable Shearing Frames, and I was desired by my men to . . . give you fair warning to pull them down, and for that purpose . . . you will take notice that if they are not taken down by the end of next week, I shall detach one of my lieutenants with at least 300 men to destroy them, and . . . we will increase your misfortunes by burning your buildings down to ashes, and if you have the impudence to fire at any of my men, they have orders to murder you . . . have the goodness to go to your neighbours and inform them that the same Fate awaits them if their Frames are not taken down . . .
>
> Signed by the General of the Army of Redressers
NED LUDD, Clerk
>
> (From a letter sent to a Huddersfield master, 1812. Home Office papers 40/41)

After the first 'Luddite' riots, the government passed a law which meant the death penalty could be passed on those found guilty of machine breaking.

There were other causes of unemployment and distress too. The prices of most goods after 1815 rose much faster than the wages of most workers. At the same time, there were thousands of soldiers and sailors returning home after the war, all looking for jobs.

The Corn Law, 1815

The attitude of the government towards these problems did nothing to help. Lord Liverpool, Prime Minister from 1812 to 1827, headed a Tory Government made up of landowners who showed little concern for the distress of working people. In 1815, Parliament passed the Corn Law. This prevented any foreign wheat (usually much cheaper than British wheat) from being imported into Britain, unless the price of British wheat was at least 80 shillings a quarter (£4 for about 13 kg). The Act aimed to keep the price of British wheat high, to ensure a good profit for landowners. The government ignored the fact that it would also mean dearer bread

– the staple food of most working people. The Corn Law naturally aroused great resentment:

> ...a series of disturbances commenced with the introduction of the Corn Bill, and continued with short intervals, until the close of the year 1816. In London and Westminster riots ensued, and were continued for several days, whilst the bill was discussed. At Bridgeport there were riots on account of the high price of bread ... at Newcastle-on-Tyne, by colliers and others; at Glasgow, where blood was shed, on account of the soup kitchens; at Preston, by unemployed weavers; at Nottingham, by Luddites ... at Merthyr Tydville, on a reduction of wages ... and December 7th, 1816, at Dundee, where, owing to the high price of meal, upwards of one hundred shops were plundered.
>
> (Samuel Bamford, *Passages in the Life of a Radical*, 2nd edition, 1840, p. 6)

(For further details on the Corn Law, see Chapter 3, page 32 and Chapter 8.)

George Cruikshank, a famous political cartoonist of the time, expressed the feelings of most people in this cartoon. It shows landowners preventing cheap French corn from being landed. The starving family say the only solution is to emigrate.

The Blessings of Peace or the Curse of the Corn Bill

Taxes

In 1816, income tax was abolished. It had been intended as a temporary measure in 1797, to help pay for the war against France. In its place, the government raised money by indirect taxes on goods which people bought:

> Taxes upon every article which enters the mouth, or covers the back, or is placed under the foot – on everything that comes from abroad or is grown at home – taxes on the raw material – taxes on every fresh value that is added to it by the industry of man – on the ermine which decorates the judge, and the rope which hangs the criminal – on the poor man's salt and the rich man's spice – on the brass nails of the coffin, and the ribands of the bride . . . *we must pay.*
> (Sydney Smith, *The Edinburgh Review*, 1820)

All sorts of everyday goods used by most people were now taxed – candles, soap, tea, tobacco and sugar – and they therefore became more expensive. Working people found themselves paying more tax, while the rich no longer had to bear the burden of income tax.

QUESTIONS

1. *Why do you think the Tory Government was opposed to working people forming themselves into Trades Unions?*
2. *(a) Find as many pieces of evidence as you can to show that hand-loom weavers had a much higher standard of living than most other working people in the late eighteenth century.*
 (b) What caused them to fall into poverty?
3. *(a) Why did the Luddites object to the introduction of new machinery?*
 (b) What is your opinion of the government's punishment for machine breaking? (Compare it with the punishment such a crime might receive today, for example.)
4. *(a) For what reason did Members of Parliament introduce the Corn Law in 1815?*
 (b) What was the objection of working people to the Corn Law?
 (c) How did they show their opposition to the Corn Law? Why did they have to resort to such violent measures?
5. *(a) List the kinds of goods taxed by the government after 1815.*
 (b) Why did working people prefer income tax to taxation of these goods?

The Radicals and Popular Protest

The Radicals

There were only two political parties represented in Parliament in the early nineteenth century – the Tories, who formed the government until as late as 1830, and the Whigs. Both these parties represented land-owning interests. Most working and middle class people were not entitled to vote for Members of Parliament in a General Election, which meant that Parliament, did not represent the interests of the great mass of the British population. (See Chapter 4.)

Many people who protested at the troubles of the time – unemployment, working conditions, taxation, and the Corn Law – were referred to as Radicals. They belonged to various groups and societies, in different parts of Britain, but were by no means united. One of the best-known Radical leaders was William Cobbett. Born a peasant's son in Surrey, he became a journalist and in 1802 founded the *Weekly Political Register*. Cobbett opposed the great changes taking place at the time – the factories in the towns and the enclosures in the countryside. In 1816, he began to publish a twopenny edition of the *Political Register*, which greatly increased its readership. (It had previously cost a shilling.)

> At this time the writings of William Cobbett suddenly became of great authority; they were read on nearly every cottage hearth in the manufacturing districts of South Lancashire; in those of Leicester, Derby, and Nottingham; also in many of the Scottish manufacturing towns. Their influence was speedily visible; he directed his readers to the true cause of their sufferings . . .
> (Samuel Bamford, *Passages in the Life of a Radical*, ed. Henry Dunckley, London 1893, p. 6)

In his 'Twopenny Trash', as the *Political Register* became known, Cobbett attacked the government, and spelled out what was needed to deal with the grievances of the people.

> The *remedy* is what we now have to look to, and that remedy consists wholly and solely of such a *reform* in the Commons' or People's House of Parliament, as shall give to every payer of *direct taxes* a vote at elections, and as shall cause the Members to be *elected annually* . . .
> ('Address to the Journeymen and Labourers', in Cobbett's *Weekly Political Register*, 2, November 1816)

The reform of Parliament was an aim shared by most Radicals. Meanwhile, working people protested against the many injustices under which they suffered. Sometimes this was done in an orderly way, sometimes not. In any case, it was bound to lead to conflict with the government, and it soon did.

The Spa Fields meeting, 1816

There had already been riots and machine breaking in protest against widespread unemployment, when a mass meeting was held in December 1816 at Spa Fields, London. It was organised by the Spencean Philanthropists, the followers of Thomas Spence. Their main aim was land reform, to take the land away from wealthy landlords and put it in the hands of all those living on the land in each parish. The Spenceans wanted the famous Radical, Henry 'Orator' Hunt to address the meeting. He agreed, but he would speak only on the subject of universal male suffrage, that is, a vote for all adult males. But matters got out of hand:

> At the close of the year, a popular meeting took place in Spa-fields, Islington, and the resolutions of reform, suggested by Mr. Henry Hunt, were voted by acclamation. The rioters, parading the streets, carried off fire-arms from the shops of several gunsmiths . . .
> (*Memoirs of the Rt.Hon.The Earl of Liverpool*, 1827)

The mob marching on the City of London was easily broken up by an armed force collected by the Mayor. However, the government was very much alarmed. They feared that bloody revolution might break out in Britain, as had happened in France after 1789, and took measures to prevent this happening:

> On the 24th [of February, 1817] a motion was made by Lord Sidmouth [Home Secretary] in the Upper House, for a suspension of the Habeas Corpus Act until the 1st of July ensuing . . . Lord Liverpool remarked, that, 'They had, according to their report, proofs of a system to overthrow the constitution of the country . . . on these grounds he asked, for a very short time, the powers which were indispensable to the salvation of the State.'
> (*Memoirs of the Rt.Hon.The Earl of Liverpool*, 1827)

The suspension of *Habeas Corpus* meant that troublesome Radicals could now be arrested on suspicion, without a specific charge being brought against them. They could then be held in custody without being brought to trial immediately – a convenient way of keeping them out of action.

Faced with arrest, Cobbett fled to America in 1817, and from there he continued to organise the publication of the *Political Register*. Meanwhile, other Radical papers became more influential, especially *The Black Dwarf*. Edited by Thomas Wooler, it sarcastically 'praised' the government for its unpopular measures. It lasted until 1824.

The 'Blanketeers' march, 1817

Unemployed Manchester workers organised a protest march to London in 1817 to present a petition to the Prince Regent, demanding the reform of Parliament and the return of the Habeas Corpus Act. They gathered at St. Peter's Fields, Manchester, before starting out. Samuel Bamford, Lancashire weaver, poet and Radical, recollected the scene:

> I endeavoured to show them that the authorities of Manchester were not likely to permit their leaving the town in a body, with blankets and petitions, as they proposed; that they could not subsist on the road; that the cold and wet would kill numbers of them . . . that many persons might join their ranks who were not reformers but enemies to reform, hired perhaps to bring them and their cause into disgrace . . . Many of the individuals were observed to have blankets, rugs, or large coats, rolled up and tied, knapsack like, on their backs . . . The appearance of these misdirected people was calculated to excite in considerable minds pity rather than resentment. Some appeared to have strength in their limbs and pleasure in their features, others already with doubt in their looks and hesitation in their steps. A few were decently clothed and well appointed for the journey; many were covered only by rags . . . and were damped by a gentle but chilling rain.
> (Samuel Bamford, *Passages in the Life of a Radical*, pp. 31–35.)

Troops broke up this meeting and pursued those who did start the march as far as Macclesfield, where most of the marchers decided to turn back.

> Few were those who marched the following morning. About a score arrived at Leek, and six only were known to pass Ashborne Bridge. And so ended the Blanket Expedition!
> (Bamford, *Passages in the Life of a Radical*)

Only one man got as far as London, and presented his petition, not to the Prince Regent, but to Lord Sidmouth. Most of the leaders were arrested, though it was doubtful if they had committed any crime. Some spent five months in prison without ever being brought to trial.

The Derbyshire rebellion

The Home Secretary, Lord Sidmouth, had no proper police force which might discover plots for overthrowing the government or bringing about reform of Parliament. He therefore made use of agents who were supposed to report to the government news of any such plots. These investigators, or *agents provocateurs* as they were known, often went far beyond reporting on the activities of Radicals and other malcontents, and went out of their way to encourage them. In 1817 Jeremiah Brandreth and a group of followers in Derbyshire, mainly unemployed textile workers, tried to seize Nottingham Castle with the encouragement of one of the most infamous of government spies, a Mr. Oliver:

> It appears that almost immediately after the suppression of the United Societies, established in different towns in this district for affecting a reform of Parliament, some of the most violent members associated together, in a private and clandestine manner. At these meetings, it is supposed to have become a question for deliberation, whether a change in the representation might not be affected without the intervention of Parliament, and a project . . . appears to have been communicated to them by a Mr. Oliver . . . This person is said to have represented to these credulous men, that all the people in the Metropolis were favourable to a complete change in the government . . . and that it was absolutely settled, that on the night . . . [of the 8th June] . . . a general rising would take place.
> (*The Mercury*, Leeds, 14 June 1817)

Acting on Oliver's information, troops arrested Brandreth and his men. Brandreth and two others were hanged, fourteen others were transported, and others imprisoned.

'Peterloo', 1819

Increasing unemployment in 1819 led to even more agitation for parliamentary reform, and to even more savage measures by the government to suppress it. Workers from all over the Manchester area gathered at St. Peter's Fields, Manchester, on 16 August 1819, to demand reform of Parliament, and to listen to Radical speakers such as Henry Hunt. In all, there were about 80 000 people, some carrying banners with slogans such as 'Liberty or Death', 'Votes for All', and 'No Corn Law'. Samuel Bamford described what happened:

> . . . We had frequently been taunted by the press with our ragged, dirty

appearance at these assemblages; with the confusion of our proceedings, and the mob-like crowds in which our numbers were mustered; and we determined that, for once at least, these reflections should not be deserved – that we would disarm the bitterness of our political opponents by a display of cleanliness, sobriety, and decorum, such as we had never before exhibited . . .

. . . Mr. Hunt . . . added . . . 'peace' . . . Order in our movements was obtained by drilling; and peace . . . was secured by a prohibition of all weapons . . . Thus our arrangements . . . were soon rendered perfect and ten thousand men moved with the regularity of ten score . . .

Our whole column, with the Rochdale people, would probably consist of six thousand men. At our head were a hundred or two of women, mostly young wives . . . A hundred or two of our handsomest girls . . . danced to the music, or sung snatches of popular songs; a score or two of children were sent back, though some went forward; whilst on each side of our line walked some thousands of stragglers. And thus . . . we went slowly towards Manchester.

. . . The meeting was indeed a tremendous one. Hunt mounted the hustings; the music ceased . . . Mr. Hunt . . . took off his white hat, and addressed the people.

. . . a noise and strange murmur arose . . . Some persons said it was the Blackburn people coming; and I stood on tiptoe . . . and saw a party of cavalry in blue and white uniform, come trotting sword in hand . . . to the front of a row of new houses, where they reined up in a line . . .

. . . On the cavalry drawing up they were received with a shout of goodwill, as I understood it . . .

(Bamford, *Passages in the Life of a Radical*)

The 'cavalry' were the Manchester Yeomanry, a body of local volunteers. They had been called out by the magistrates who had been advised by Lord Sidmouth that any such demonstrations should be severely dealt with. Hunt offered to give himself up to the magistrates, but was allowed by them to continue. Then he was seized by soldiers in the middle of his speech. When there was an uproar around Hunt, the magistrates believed the crowd were attacking the soldiers. They ordered the cavalry to disperse the crowd, with terrible results:

. . . they dashed forward, and began cutting the people.

. . . and their sabres were plied to hew a way through naked held-up hands, and defenceless heads; and then chopped limbs, and wound-gaping

Peterloo

skulls were seen; and groans and cries were mingled with the din of that horrid confusion . . .

On the breaking of the crowd, the yeomanry wheeled; and dashing wherever there was an opening, they followed, pressing and wounding. Many females appeared as the crowd opened; and striplings or mere youths were also found . . . Women, white-vested maids, and tender youths, were indiscriminately sabred or trampled . . .

(Bamford, *Passages in the Life of a Radical*)

Eleven people were killed and about 400 seriously injured, including many women and children. Hunt was sentenced to two years' imprisonment, and the magistrates were congratulated on their work by Lord Sidmouth. Throughout Britain, there was a tremendous outcry against the government, and the 'victory' was scornfully referred to as the 'Battle of Peterloo'.

The government's reaction – the 'Six Acts', 1819

There had been nothing illegal about the meeting at St. Peter's Fields. However, the government wanted to prevent similar meetings taking place and to counteract the growing movement for parliamentary reform. As a result, Sidmouth quickly drew up new laws which Parliament passed in December, 1819, a few months after the 'Peterloo' massacre. These were the infamous 'Six Acts'.

1 . . .
Whereas, in some parts of the U.K., men clandestinely and unlawfully assembled have practised military training and exercise, to the great terror and alarm of H.M.'s peaceable and loyal subjects . . . be it therefore enacted . . . that all meetings . . . for the purpose of training or drilling . . . are hereby prohibited.

2 . . .
Whereas arms and weapons of various sorts have in many parts of this Kingdom been collected, and are kept for purposes dangerous to the public peace . . . be it therefore enacted . . . that it shall be lawful for any J.P. . . . that he . . . believe that any pike, pikehead or spear . . . dirk, dagger, pistol, gun or other weapon is . . . in the possession of any person, or in any house or place, to issue his warrant . . . to search for and seize such . . . weapon . . .

3 . . .
Whereas great delays have occurred in the administration of justice . . . by reason that the defendants in some of the said cases have, according to the present practice . . . an opportunity of postponing their trials to a distant period . . . be it enacted . . . that [such persons] . . . shall be required to plead . . . within four days from the time of his or her appearance.

4 . . .
Whereas . . . assemblies of large numbers of persons collected from various parishes and districts . . . have of late been held . . . Be it enacted . . . that no meeting of any description of persons, exceeding the number of 50 . . . shall be holden . . . unless in the parish . . . within which the persons calling any such meeting shall usually . . . dwell.

5 . . .
Be it enacted . . . that . . . in every case in which any verdict . . . shall be had against any person for composing, printing or publishing any blasphemous libel . . . it shall be lawful . . . to make an order for the seizure . . . [of] all

copies of the libel . . . and . . . for any Justice . . . to search for any copies of such libel in any house or other place . . .

6 . . .

Whereas pamphlets and printed papers containing observations . . . tending to excite hatred . . . of the Government . . . have lately been published in great numbers, and at very small prices . . . be it enacted . . . that . . . all pamphlets and papers containing any public news . . . printed in the U.K. for sale . . . for a less sum than sixpence . . . shall be deemed . . . newspapers . . . and be subject to . . . the same duties of stamps . . . as newspapers . . .
(*Statutes at Large*, LXXIV, pp. 1–42)

These laws were a tremendous blow to the Radical movement. Mass meetings could no longer be held, and it was now extremely risky to publish or even to read a Radical newspaper such as the *Political Register* or *Black Dwarf*.

The Cato Street conspiracy, 1820

Throughout Britain, people were shocked at 'Peterloo' and the restrictions on individual freedom imposed by the 'Six Acts'. In retaliation, Arthur Thistlewood, a Spencean Philanthropist, and some friends planned in their Cato Street headquarters in London to kill all the Cabinet ministers in a single night.

It had been ascertained by the gang, that the greater part of his majesty's ministers were to dine together at the Earl of Harrowby's, and this was considered a favourable opportunity for effecting their entire extermination: Thistlewood was to have knocked at Lord Harrowby's door, with a letter . . . or with a red box, such as is used in all the public offices, desiring it to be delivered immediately to the cabinet ministers at dinner, without delay . . . Thistlewood, with another of the conspirators, entered the hall as if to wait. They were immediately to open the street door, others were to come in with hand-grenades, which were to be thrown into the house . . . in the confusion . . . all the rest of the conspirators were to rush into the dining-room . . . and the work of assassination was to have been instantly begun.
(G.T. Williams, *An Authentic History of the Cato Street Conspiracy*, 1820)

After the assassinations, Thistlewood hoped to seize London, but a government spy, Edwards, had helped with the plan and passed on the information to the authorities. Thistlewood and his fellow plotters were arrested in their Cato Street hideout before they could even begin to carry out their plan. Thistlewood and four others were hanged and beheaded, and six others were transported for life to Botany Bay in Australia.

'Death or Liberty!' (The Tory view of the Radicals)

The 'Radical War', 1820

In the Spring of 1820, striking weavers in Glasgow and nearby towns such as Paisley attempted a rebellion. There was a general strike in Glasgow, and the 'Radical Address' was seen in many towns of central Scotland.

ADDRESS
TO THE
INHABITANTS OF GREAT BRITAIN & IRELAND

FRIENDS AND COUNTRYMEN,

ROUSED from that torpid state in which WE have been sunk for so many years, We are at length compelled, from the extremity of our sufferings, and the contempt heaped upon our Petitions for redress, to assert our RIGHTS, at the hazard of our lives, which (if not misrepresented by designing men, would have United all ranks) have reduced us to take up ARMS for the redress of our Common Grievances.

. . .

Our principles are few, and founded on the basis of our CONSTITU-TION, which were purchased with the DEAREST BLOOD of our AN-CESTORS, and which we swear to transmit to posterity unsullied, or PERISH in the Attempt. – Equality of Rights (not of Property), is the object for which we contend; and which we consider as the only security for our LIBERTIES and LIVES.

Let us show the world that We are not that Lawless, Sanguinary Rabble, which our Oppressors would persuade the higher circles we are – but a BRAVE and GENEROUS PEOPLE, determined to be FREE. LIBERTY or DEATH is our Motto, and We have sworn to return home in triumph – or return no more!

By the order of the Committee of Organisation,
for forming a PROVISIONAL GOVERNMENT
GLASGOW, 1st April, 1820.

(Rozelle MSS)

Only a very few workers actually took up arms. One group, led by John Baird and Andrew Hardie, marched on the Carron Works near Falkirk, but government agents had again been involved in the plan, and troops of the 10th Hussars and the Stirlingshire Yeomanry defeated the rebels in a skirmish at Bonnymuir. Another group, led by James Wilson, marched on Glasgow but found no support there, and Wilson was arrested. Wilson, Hardie and Baird were all executed.

The Queen Caroline affair, 1820

George III died in 1820, and was succeeded by his son, the Prince Regent, who now became George IV. The new king had first been married in secret to a Mrs Fitzherbert, but this marriage was never legally recognised. Then in 1795, under pressure from his family, he unwillingly married Princess Caroline of Brunswick, but they separated soon after their daughter, Charlotte, was born. Now Caroline returned to claim her crown. Because of her involvement in many scandalous affairs, she was completely unacceptable to George and to the government. The government introduced a Bill of Pains and Penalties to dissolve the marriage, but met with tremendous opposition from the public, who felt Caroline had been wronged. The Radicals took the opportunity of supporting Caroline's claim to be Queen as a means of attacking the government. During an investigation of Caroline's past (required for the Bill of Pains and Penalties) she received this declaration of support from the workers of Manchester:

> Your Majesty cannot be unacquainted with the severe privations and deep sufferings of this immense population; and doubtless your Majesty's benevolent heart has been wrung at the dreadful events of the fateful 16th August. The same power which scourged us is now oppressing you; – it is not less our interest than our duty, therefore, to stand up against your Majesty's enemies, who are also the enemies of the rights and liberties of the whole people.
> ('Address to the Most Gracious Majesty the Queen from the Artisans, Mechanics, and Labouring Classes of the Town of Manchester'; in Cobbett's *Weekly Political Register*, 30 September 1820)

Caroline replied:

> I receive with great satisfaction this loyal, affectionate, and impressive Address, from so numerous, so useful, and so efficient a part of the community . . . The true honour of the country has in the highest degree been promoted by their incomparable skill . . . I am happy to perceive that the industrious classes in the town of Manchester, as well as in the rest of the kingdom, regard the unconstitutional attack upon my rights as an illegal invasion of their own. The Bill of Pains and Penalties . . . weakens the security of that sacred tenure by which every Briton is protected in his liberty, his property, and his life.
> (Cobbett, *Weekly Political Register*, 30 September 1820)

Faced with such controversy, the government dropped the Bill of Pains and Penalties. Caroline presented herself at George IV's coronation at Westminster Abbey, but was refused admittance! She accepted a government pension to drop her claim and died in 1821.

QUESTIONS

The Radicals

1   Why did William Cobbett's influence as a Radical leader increase in 1816?
2   What was the central aim of all Radicals, as stated by William Cobbett in his

Political Register? *Why did so many working and middle class people support this aim?*

3 *Why did Radicals believe that other reforms – abolition of the Corn Law, factory reform, relief for the unemployed and so on – would follow the achievement of this aim?*

Peaceful protests ...

1 What was the purpose of mass demonstrations such as the Spa Fields meeting of 1816, the 'Blanketeers' march in 1817, and the St. Peter's Fields meeting in 1819? Were the people involved breaking the law in holding such demonstrations?

2 Look at the document extracts on the 'Blanketeers'. What evidence is there that this march had little chance of success?

3 Look at the 'Peterloo' extracts. List all the information you can find to show that this was intended to be a peaceful meeting.

4 For what reason did the Manchester workers (and Radicals in general) support the cause of Caroline of Brunswick? (Was it because they thought she would be a suitable Queen?)

... And violent ones

1 (a) Describe the violent methods used, or attempted, in each of the following: (i) the Derbyshire rebellion. (ii) the 'Radical War'. (iii) the Cato Street conspiracy.
(b) Can you think of any reason why the people involved in these three incidents should have resorted to violence, rather than use peaceful methods? (Consider how the government reacted to cases of peaceful protest.)

Government measures

1 What did the suspension of the Habeas Corpus Act allow the government to do? How could the suspension of this Act cause an innocent person to suffer?

2 Describe, in each case, how the government treated: (i) the people at the Spa Fields meeting in 1816. (ii) the 'Blanketeers'. (iii) the people at the St. Peter's Fields meeting in 1819. Did the government have any justification for its actions in any of these cases? Give reasons for your answer.

3 How did government spies such as Mr. Oliver go about getting convictions?

4 (a) Make a list of the 'Six Acts' using your own words.

(*b*) (*i*) *Which of these Acts would probably be supported by any government which wanted to keep the peace?* (*ii*) *Which of the Acts unfairly restricted the freedom of the people to criticise their government?*
(*c*) *How did these Acts hinder the Radical movement?*

ASSIGNMENTS

A. *Imagine you were a person living and working either in the town or the country immediately after 1815. Write a letter to a friend abroad about the troubles you and your family face under Lord Liverpool's government.*
B. *Write an article for William Cobbett's* Political Register *criticising government policies, and putting forward Radical ideas.*
C. *Imagine you were present at St. Peters Fields, Manchester, on August 16, 1819. Write an account of what happened that day, and your opinions on how the meeting was handled by the magistrates and troops.*
D. *Prepare arguments* for *and* against *the methods used by the government to suppress protest and criticism after 1815.*

3 The Liberal Tories

From 1822–30, the Tories still formed the government, and Lord Liverpool remained Prime Minister until 1827. He was followed by George Canning and then Lord Goderich, who each lasted in office for only a few months. From 1828–30 the Prime Minister was the Duke of Wellington.

Before 1822, as we have seen in Chapter 2, the Tory Government opposed all reform. There were newcomers to the government, however, who helped to change the Tory Party's approach to governing the country. These new men were known as 'Liberal Tories' because they were prepared to carry out reforms where they saw a need for them. One of the new men who made important changes was William Huskisson, President of the Board of Trade. He was specially interested in Britain's trade with overseas countries. At this time, manufacturers in the large industrial towns wanted to improve their trade with other countries by changing the laws on imports and exports. With the help of Frederick Robinson, Chancellor of the Exchequer, Huskisson began moves to make Britain a 'free trade' country.

Another new man was Robert Peel, the son of a rich cotton factory owner, who entered Parliament at the age of twenty-one. He was Chief Secretary for Ireland from 1812–18, and was promoted to Home Secretary in 1822. As Home Secretary, Peel was responsible for upholding law and order in Britain.

(For other reforms of the Liberal Tories, see: Chapter 4 – how the laws which prevented people of certain religious beliefs from becoming members of Parliament were changed; Chapter 7 – how the laws dealing with Trade Unions were changed; and Chapter 8 – how import duties were reduced further under the 'free trade' movement.)

First Steps towards Free Trade

Import duties were charged on nearly all goods brought into Britain until the 1820s. The intention was to limit the amount of imports, and most other countries operated the same system. Manufacturers had originally been in favour of such duties:

. . . it is the interest of the merchants and the manufacturers of every country to secure to themselves the monopoly of the home market. Hence in Great Britain, and in most other European countries, the extraordinary duties upon almost all goods imported by alien merchants. Hence the high duties and prohibitions upon all those foreign manufactures which can come into competition with our own.

(Adam Smith, *An Enquiry into the Nature and Causes of the Wealth of Nations*, E. Cannon (ed.) vol. 1, p. 458, 4th edition, 1925)

However, Britain was the first country in the world to mass-produce goods in factories. Soon more goods could be produced than the people of Britain required. Manufacturers now wanted to export their surplus goods with as little restriction as possible. Lord Liverpool said:

. . . it was perfectly clear that every nation ought to be left to prosecute without interference that particular species of industry for which . . . it was in all respects best adapted. Each nation could then purchase whatever commodities it might require, from those quarters where they could be raised and brought home at the cheapest rate, and of the best quality. If that system were to be adopted by all the considerable nations of the world, there could be no doubt but that it was the system which all must consider as the most proper and most desirable.

(Hansard, *Parliamentary Debates*, vol. XXX, 1815, col. 177)

Huskisson and Robinson shared the new ideas on freedom of trade, and set out to remove where possible those laws which restricted Britain's exports. In 1822–3 they reduced the duty on many imported goods, such as rum, silk, cotton and linen goods, wool, china, glass, metals and paper. The duty on manufactured goods was lowered from 50 to 20 per cent, and on raw materials, from 20 to 10 per cent. In 1823, the Reciprocity of Duties Act was passed. This said that Britain would reduce the duty charged on imports from any foreign country, if that country would in return reduce its own duty on British goods. The Navigation Acts had insisted on Britain's imports and exports being carried in British ships, but from the 1820s onwards these Acts were disregarded more and more.

The Corn Law of 1815 was added to the system of import duties. (See Chapter 2.) It was supposed to prevent cheap foreign wheat entering Britain, so that the landowners could sell their wheat at a high price. Since this meant that bread would cost more, working people naturally opposed the Corn Law. So did middle class factory owners, for (among other reasons) high priced bread meant they had to pay higher wages.

> Were it not for these restraints [the Corn Law], we might be able to purchase the same amount of bread of 40*s*. or at most 50*s*., that now costs 70*s*. or 80*s* . . . By permitting the free importation of foreign corn no real injury would be done to the landlords; for assuredly they have no right to be benefited at the expense of the other classes. It is the duty of Government . . . not certainly to give undue advantages to any one class at the expense of the rest.
> (*The Scotsman*, 6 May 1820)

Most Members of Parliament at this time were landowners who feared that repealing the Corn Law would bring cheap corn into Britain and ruin them. Foreign corn was not allowed into Britain until the price of homegrown wheat had reached eighty shillings a quarter (about £4 per 13 kg). Huskisson could not abolish the Corn Law but he did alter it, using the 'Sliding Scale' of 1828. Now, as British corn became more expensive, the duty on imported corn was lowered until foreign corn could enter Britain duty free when British corn was 74s a quarter.

QUESTIONS

1 (a) *Why did British manufacturers originally want high import duties to limit the amount of foreign goods entering Britain?*
(b) *What made manufacturers change their minds and support free trade?*
2 (a) *Make a list of Huskisson's measures to help Free Trade.*
(b) *How would these measures help (i) British manufacturers, (ii) working people in Britain?*
3 (a) *What change was made to the Corn Law in 1828?*
(b) *Why did Huskisson not completely abolish the Corn Law at that time?*

ASSIGNMENTS

A. *Write speeches presenting the argument* for *Free Trade from the point of view of (a) a British factory worker, and (b) a British factory owner.*
B. *Write a speech presenting the argument* against *Free Trade from the point of view of a British landowner.*

Law and Order in the Early Nineteenth Century

Enforcing the law

The task of keeping law and order seemed an impossible one, since crime was increasing at an alarming rate, especially in the new industrial towns and cities. Britain had no properly organised police force until Robert Peel established the Metropolitan Police in 1829. Before then a few full-time police officers were attached to police stations. In each parish, there was a parish constable who was responsible for keeping law and order. Watchmen also patrolled the streets at night. They were called 'Charleys' since the force of watchmen had been greatly enlarged during the reign of Charles II (1660–85). The 'Bow Street Runners' was a force founded in the early eighteenth century and based in Bow Street, London. 'Thief-takers' informed on and handed over criminals, but they were only interested in receiving rewards and were often as dishonest as the people they turned in.

These unco-ordinated arrangements could not cope with the huge increase in crime in the industrial areas.

> *Watchmen*
> ... In 1810, there were only three watchmen in Preston ... At this time, the streets were guarded, at night, by watchmen, who used to shout out the hours and half hours, and announce the state of the weather. At intervals they esconced themselves in wooden sentry-like boxes, which stood on small wheels. These boxes were stationed in different parts of the town to suit the beats of the watchmen.
> (A. Hewitson, *A History of Preston*, p. 332, *Chronicle* office, Preston, 1883)

> [The Watchmen], being selected for the office on account of excessive age and extraordinary infirmity, had a custom of shutting themselves up tight in their boxes on the first symptoms of disturbance, and remaining there until they disappeared.
> (Charles Dickens, *Barnaby Rudge*, p. 297)

> *A Policeman's earnings*
> Are you accustomed to receive compensation from private individuals, who employ you on any specific service ... ? – *Yes; and that is the only means by which we can exist.*

If it were not for that reward . . . should you consider the salary paid by the public as sufficient . . . ? – *Certainly not; I could not do it* . . .

Do you receive in cases of convictions or apprehensions of offenders . . . a share in that reward which is known by the name of the Parliamentary reward? – *I have received several shares.*

The Committee are to understand, that if you ever had any information against . . . a person, and knew where to find him, you would take him into custody? – *I can lay my hand on my heart and say I would immediately.*

Whether the offence for which he was taken would be productive of great reward or small? – *Certainly; how can an officer calculate upon what he would be worth if he was left.*

(Evidence of a police officer in 1816 to the Select Committee, Police of the Metropolis, *Parliamentary Papers*, 1816, v., pp. 146–7)

QUESTIONS

1   *What evidence is there to show that watchmen were unlikely to have much success in catching criminals?*
2   *(a) In what ways was the policeman paid for his work?*
  (b) Would the system of rewards make for better or worse police officers? Give reasons for your answer.
  (c) In the last extract, what suspicions does the questioner have about the rewards system?

The new police

In an attempt to improve law and order, Peel introduced the Metropolitan Police Act in 1829. A full-time police force based at Scotland Yard in London was created by the Act. This force at first consisted of 3000 paid constables armed only with staves. Their duty was to arrest criminals in an area of approximately 20 kilometres radius of Charing Cross in central London. They were so successful that many criminals fled from London, and police forces like the London one were set up in other parts of the country.

Recruiting Procedure
If . . . who has applied for a SITUATION AS CONSTABLE IN THE POLICE; will attend at . . . Westminster, on . . . next . . . at . . . o'clock in the . . . precisely, he will be examined as to his fitness for such an employment. He need not attend, and will not be appointed, if he cannot read or

write; if he is above thirty-five years of age; if he is under 5 feet, 7 inches high without his shoes; nor unless he is free from any bodily complaint, of a strong constitution, and generally intelligent; as he will have to pass the strict examination of the surgeon.

N.B. The applicant will not be examined without producing this notice, and two letters of recommendation to the Commissioners of Police, from respectable housekeepers, and a recommendation from his last employer.

(The Select Committee on Metropolitan Police, *Parliamentary Papers*, 1834, xvi, p. 6)

Peelers

The 'Beat' system

During the night, they never cease patrolling the whole time they are on duty . . . To every beat certain constables are specifically assigned, and they are provided with little maps called beat-cards . . . So thoroughly is this arrangement carried into effect, that every street, road, alley, lane and court, within the Metropolitan Police District is visited constantly day and night by some of the police . . . in those parts of the town which are open and inhabited by the wealthier classes, an occasional visit from a policeman is sufficient . . . But the limits of the beat are diminished, and of course the frequency of the visits increased, in proportion to the character and density of the population . . . the concentration of property, and the intricacy of the streets . . . there are points which, in fact, are never free from inspection.

. . . In a case of emergency, the Commissioners could communicate intelligence to every man in the force, and collect the whole 5500 men in one place in two hours.

(*Edinburgh Review*, July 1852; pp. 8–10)

QUESTIONS

1 (*a*) *Why were the standards of health and fitness for a policeman so strict?*
  (*b*) *Why did a police recruit have to produce two letters when he applied to join the force?*
2 (*a*) *Why would the 'Beat' system discourage criminals?*
  (*b*) *Can you think of any advantage the regular police patrols might give criminals?*
  (*c*) *Which areas were patrolled most frequently, and why?*
3 *Why would the Commissioners want to gather together all, or a large part of, the Metropolitan Police force very rapidly at one point? (See Chapter 2, and the events of the period 1815–22.)*

Public opinion and the new police

At first, many people doubted the usefulness of the new police force. (See cartoon p. 38.) Others feared the use the government might make of Peel's police. A leaflet distributed in London tried to rouse feeling against the police:

> Liberty or Death! Britons! and Honest Men!!! The Time has at last arrived. All London meets on Tuesday. We assure you that 6000 cutlasses have been removed from the Tower for the use of Peel's Bloody Gang. These damned Police are now to be armed. Englishmen, will you put up with this?
> (Charles Reith *A New Study of Police History*, Oliver & Boyd, 1956 p. 155)

Peel defended his new force and tried to win over the public:

> *5 November 1829*
> I want to teach people that liberty does not consist of having your home robbed by organised gangs of thieves, and in leaving the principal streets of London in the nightly possession of drunken women and vagabonds.
> (Letter from Peel to Wellington in C.S Parker (ed) *Sir Robert Peel*, vol. II, 1899)

A THUNDERING PEEL TO THIEVES PICKPOCKETS WATCHMEN, &c. &c.

Good standards of behaviour were expected from policemen:

> He will be civil and attentive to all persons, of every rank and class: insolence and incivility will not be passed over. He must remember that there is no qualification more indispensable to a Police Officer than a perfect command of temper, never suffering himself to be moved in the slightest degree, by any language or threats that might be used: if he do his duty in a quiet and determined manner, such conduct will probably induce well-disposed bystanders to assist him should he require it. (Reith, *op. cit.* p. 140)

In spite of initial opposition to the new police force, it quickly became popular. Police officers were nicknamed 'Peelers' and 'Bobbies' after their founder.

QUESTIONS

1   What did the public think of Peel's new police force at first? (Look at the cartoon 'A Thundering Peel . . .' above.)

2   (a) What arguments were used against the new police?
(b) Why might people be suspicious of a properly organised police force? (See Chapter 2, especially the section 'The Radicals and Popular Protest'.)

3   How did Peel try to counter these fears and suspicions?

ASSIGNMENTS

A. *Imagine that the year is 1820. Write a letter to the authorities complaining about the amount of crime in the cities, and demanding better law and order.*

B. *Present the arguments for and against the new police forces after 1829. Which side would you have taken? (Give reasons for your answer.)*

Reform of the Penal Code

Parliament introduced increasingly severe punishments to try to discourage criminals from committing crimes. By the early nineteenth century, there were over 200 crimes punishable by death. These included the serious crimes of treason, rebellion and murder, but also less serious ones, such as stealing goods worth more than two pounds, cutting down trees, sending threatening letters and sheep-stealing. You could even be put to death for damaging Westminster Bridge or impersonating a Chelsea Pensioner! Executions were still being carried out in public. (The last public execution was in 1868.)

Opinions of the Law
... Shopkeepers of the highest respectability, had stated cases in which they had submitted to considerable loss, being deterred from prosecution by the belief that the punishment was infinitely beyond what humanity and expediency required ...
(The Marquis of Lansdowne, House of Commons, 17 July 1820, *Hansard*, Vol 2, p. 491)

A public execution
From an early hour in the morning, the population of the surrounding districts came pouring into Bury; and the whole of the labouring classes in that town struck work for the day, in order that they might have an opportunity of witnessing the execution of this wretched criminal ... upwards of 1000 persons were assembled around the scaffold ... and their numbers kept increasing till 12 o'clock, when they amounted to at least 7000 persons.

The two attendants led him [Corder] forward to the platform ... The executioner immediately placed the cap on his head, drew it over his eyes, and then adjusted the rope ... the platform fell without any signal from the prisoner ... The executioner seized him by the knees ... while he struggled in the agonies of death ... The body was left hanging for an hour, then cut

MORAL INFLUENCE OF
EXECUTIONS

*Where ave ve bin? Why, to
see the Cove 'ung, to be
sure!*

down, and taken in a cart . . . to the Shire Hall . . . and the public were admitted to see it till the evening.
(*Sunday Times*, 17 August 1828, describing the execution of William Corder, the murderer of Maria Marten in the notorious 'Red Barn' case)

Transportation for 7 or 14 years was the punishment for lesser crimes, such as stealing turnips from a field or killing a rabbit. This meant being taken by ship to Australia or Tasmania, and the death-penalty for attempting to escape and returning home. Transportation was gradually brought to an end between 1840 and 1867.

Convicts in Australia
. . . as every kind of skilled labour is very scarce in New South Wales, a convict who has been a blacksmith, carpenter, mason, cooper, wheelwright, or gardener, is a most valuable servant . . .

The condition of convicts in the road-parties . . . appears to have been a more disagreeable one than that of assigned servants; the very nature of the work of convicts in road-parties, particularly that of breaking stones under a hot sun, was irksome . . .

The condition of the convicts in the [penal settlements] has been shown ... to be one of unmitigated wretchedness ... He [Sir Francis Forbes, the Chief-Justice of Australia] likewise mentioned the case of several men at Norfolk Island cutting the heads of their fellow prisoners with a hoe while at work, with a certainty of being detected, and with certainty of being executed.
(The Select Committee on Transportation, *Parliamentary Papers*, 1837–8, xxii, pp. v, vi, ix, xii, xv)

Convict ship

Even though the punishments for crime were very severe, crime still continued to increase. In an attempt to make the criminal code less severe and more humane, Sir Samuel Romilly and Sir James Mackintosh provided evidence which led to Peel's reform of the Penal Code in 1824. Over one hundred offences were removed from the list of crimes punishable by death. By 1828, only murder, treason and arson in the King's dockyards remained capital crimes.

QUESTIONS

1 Why did some people not want to prosecute criminals, even though they had suffered at their hands?

2 (a) What evidence is there of the popularity of public executions?

(*b*) *Why do you think executions in public had a bad effect on people?*

3   (*a*) *What does the illustration on page 41 tell you about conditions on a transportation ship?*

(*b*) *What different jobs were transported convicts given? Which were the best, and which the worst, jobs?*

(*c*) *How can you tell that transportation was a hated punishment?*

ASSIGNMENTS

A. *Why did severe punishments not stop crime increasing at the start of the nineteenth century?*

B. *What was still inhumane about the penal code by 1851?*

Prisons at the beginning of the nineteenth century

Local bodies were responsible at this time for the organisation of prisons. As a result, there were many types of prisons – county gaols, town gaols, and even private gaols belonging to some nobles and bishops. Conditions therefore varied considerably from prison to prison. Many local magistrates avoided the duty of inspecting prisons, so that conditions in most prisons were very bad.

> *Prison life*
> . . . the moment he [the prisoner] enters prison, irons are hammered on to him; then he is cast into the midst of a compound of all that is disgusting and depraved. At night he is locked up in a narrow cell, with perhaps half a dozen of the worst thieves in London, or as many vagrants, whose rags are alive, and in actual motion with vermin: he may find himself in bed, and in bodily contact, between a robber and a murderer; or between a man with a foul disease on one side, and with an infectious disorder on the other.
> (Thomas Fowell Buxton, J. and A. Arc, *An Inquiry Whether Crime and Misery are produced or prevented by our present system of Prison Discipline'*, 1818, pp. 15–17)

> Their provision was put down to them through a hole in the floor of the room above: and those who served them often caught the fatal fever. ['Gaol fever' or typhus.] At my first visit I found the keeper, his assistant, and all the prisoners but one sick of it, and heard that but a few years before, many prisoners had died of it: and the keeper and his wife in one night.
> (John Howard, *The State of the Prisons*, pp. 200–201)

Gaolers were unpaid, so they paid little attention to the welfare of their prisoners, or to keeping order in prison. They 'earned' their income by charging fees from prison inmates.

Prison discipline

At four o'clock in the afternoon in the winter, and at six o'clock in the summer, the bell rings . . . The prisoners are then issued into their day rooms, in which they continue uninspected and unemployed until seven o'clock in the winter, and eight o'clock in the summer, at which hour they are locked up in their sleeping cells. This period, as well as the greater part of the Sabbath, is devoted to noise, jollity and mirth. We were introduced to the felon's day room during these evening hours of riot and confusion. It was crowded to excess: and never have we seen a company of prisoners more marked by the appearance of turbulence and desperation.

(John Joseph Gurney, *Notes on a Visit to Some Prisons in Scotland and the North of England in Company with Elizabeth Fry*, p. 87)

There were no separate prisons for children. Prisoners of all ages were mixed together, whatever crimes they had committed.

Children in Prison

However bad a child may be previous to his entrance in Gaol, he generally feels a certain degree of terror associated with the idea of prison . . . The prison once entered, however, the little culprit finds himself surrounded by those who make him ashamed, not for what he has done, but for the little he has done. It is a melancholy truth that many young delinquents soon acquire an ambition to excel in crime.

(W.L. Clay, *The Prison Chaplain*, p. 13, 1861)

The government did provide one type of prison – the 'Hulks'. These were old naval or merchant ships no longer fit for sea, and they originally housed prisoners awaiting transportation.

Life on Board the 'Hulks'

. . . All that has been stated of the miserable effects of the association of criminals in the prisons on shore, the profaneness, the vice, the demoralisation that are its inevitable consequences, applies in its fullest extent in [the hulks] . . . The convicts, after being shut up for the night, are allowed to have lights between decks, in some ships as late as ten o'clock . . . they are permitted the use of musical instruments; . . . dancing, fighting and gaming

take place; the old offenders are in the habit of robbing the new comers; . . .
a communication is frequently kept up with their old associates on shore;
and occasionally spirits are introduced on board . . .
(Select Committee on Secondary Punishments, *Parliamentary Papers*,
1831–2, vii, pp. 12–13)

QUESTIONS

1   *Why did disease spread rapidly in prisons?*
2   *(a) How did gaolers earn a living?*
    (b) Why do you think that gaolers did not try to keep better order in prisons?
3   *Why was it such a bad thing to allow adults and children to mix freely in
    prison?*
4   *Why was discipline on board the 'hulks' so bad?*
5   *What chance do you think prisoners would have had of becoming law-abiding
    citizens after spending time in prison? Give reasons for your answer.*

Improvements in prison conditions

John Howard, the Sheriff of Bedfordshire (1726–90) carried out the first detailed
investigation into prison conditions throughout Britain. His book, *The State of
the Prisons* (1777), contained his findings on prison life.

Mrs. Elizabeth Fry had more recently inspected prisons. She was a Quaker,
and her religious beliefs had moved her to try to improve prison conditions and the
behaviour of prisoners. In 1813 she visited for the first time Newgate Gaol, in
London, one of the worst prisons in Britain. In 1817 she formed the Association
for the Improvement of Female Prisoners in Newgate. This committee of ladies
tried to improve prison conditions and to encourage prisoners to behave decently.
Eventually, disorder in the gaol lessened. Elizabeth Fry visited many other prisons, and set up many other associations like the one at Newgate. In 1818 she gave
evidence to a Parliamentary Committee, and spoke of her own ideas on prison
conditions for women:

> *Elizabeth Fry's ideal prison*
> I should prefer a prison where women were allowed to work together in
> companies with proper superintendance, and their recreation also; to have
> their meals together, under proper superintendance; . . . Their being in com-
> panies during the day tends, under proper regulation, to the advancement of

principle and industry, for it affords a stimulus. I would think solitary confinement proper only in very atrocious cases.
(John Kent, *Elizabeth Fry*, p. 80)

Mrs. Fry's prison rules
2. That the women be engaged in needlework, knitting, or any other suitable employment.
3. That there be no begging, swearing, gaming, card-playing, quarrelling, or immoral conversation . . .
10. That at the ringing of the bell, at nine o'clock in the morning, the women collect in the work-room to hear a portion of scripture read by one of the visitors, or the matron; . . .
(*Memoir of Elizabeth Fry*, vol. 1, pp. 269–70)

The effect of the scripture reading
After the reading is over, the company sits for a few minutes in perfect silence . . . the word of Scripture . . . appears to excite in prisoners much tenderness of mind; and we have sometimes observed during these periods of serious thought that almost every eye in the room has been wet with tears.
(Gurney, *Prisons in Scotland and the North of England*, p. 157)

My readings at Newgate . . . are to my feelings too much like making a show of a good thing . . .
(Elizabeth Fry after a visit to Newgate in 1818. From *Memoir of Elizabeth Fry*, vol. 1, p. 345)

QUESTIONS

1 (a) How should women prisoners have spent their time, according to Elizabeth Fry?
(b) What should they have been forbidden to do?
(c) Why was Mrs. Fry opposed to solitary confinement, in most cases?
2 (a) What effect was religious instruction supposed to have had on the prisoners?
(b) Is there any reason to doubt that this was true?

Robert Peel, the Home Secretary, now took action to improve prison conditions. His Prison Act of 1823 made the following improvements:
1. Prison buildings were to be roomy and sanitary.
2. Gaolers were to be paid, and the system of gaolers' fees was to be stopped.

3. Training was to be given to prisoners, including reading, writing and religious instruction.

4. Female warders were to supervise female prisoners.

5. Chaplains and doctors were to visit prisons regularly.

6. Permission had to be given by a Justice of the Peace for irons or chains to be used on prisoners.

The Act did not include any means of making sure it could be enforced. This was a serious fault, because it meant that the Act was ignored in many prisons, especially the smaller ones, where conditions remained as bad as before. However, if magistrates did want to improve prison conditions, they now had Peel's Act to help them. It was not until 1835 that the Home Secretary became directly responsible for prisons, and could appoint prison inspectors.

QUESTIONS

1 (a) *Make a note of the terms of Peel's Prison Act of 1823 (six points).*
   (b) *Consider what you have already found out about prison conditions before 1823. Would Peel's Act have put right all that was wrong in prisons, even if it could have been properly enforced at the time?*

ASSIGNMENTS

A. *Using all the available evidence, write an extract from a prisoner's diary, covering one or more days, at the beginning of the nineteenth century.*

B. *Make a list of improvements you feel should have been introduced, in addition to the prison reforms of the 1820s.*

4 Parliament

The Beginnings of Change

We have seen in Chapter 2 that some people were discontented with the parliamentary system of the early nineteenth century. This system dated back to the Middle Ages, when it was natural for the king to seek advice from and give favours to, the wealthiest and most important people – the landowners. Since then, however, the Industrial Revolution had led to the growth of new classes – the middle class of wealthy business owners and the factory workers. The middle class felt that their importance as leaders in the fields of industry and trade should permit them to sit in Parliament; the working class wanted people in Parliament who would pass laws to improve their living and working conditions.

The Tory Government was already involved in making prisons and the penal code more humane, and passing measures to make trading easier, under the influence of the Liberal Tories (see Chapter 3), but they were against the idea of any fundamental reform of the political system. They believed that landowners were the best people to run the country. However, before the 1820s were over, they had made a beginning to reform by removing some of the old laws which made religion a barrier to political positions. The first of these laws concerned the 'test' people had to satisfy before they could become members of local councils, or hold official positions.

Repeal of the Corporation and Test Acts

Lord John Russell has brought forward a bill for the repeal of the Corporation and Test Acts; the former of which requires that every member of a corporation [local council] and the latter all persons admitted to any office civil or military, or receiving wages from the crown, or being servants in the royal household, shall . . . file a certificate of having received the holy communion according to the rites of the Church of England . . .
The effects of the bills have long been set aside; but the Acts themselves

remain unrepealed, irritating the Dissenter [non-member of the Church of England] without benefitting the Church.
(*Christian Observer* XXVIII, 1828 p. 206)

The Tory party had always supported the Church of England, but few of its members opposed the repeal of these Acts since they had been widely ignored for a long time. The government thus accepted Lord Russell's arguments, and the result in May 1828 was:

An Act for repealing so much of several Acts as imposes the necessity of the Lord's Supper as a Qualification for certain Offices and Employments.
(Public General Statutes, 1828; in Norman Gash, *The Age of Peel*, (1968), p. 20)

Before long, however, the Tories were pushed into another change which split the party wide open. This concerned the position of Roman Catholics.

Catholic emancipation

In 1801, by the Act of Union, Ireland lost its own Parliament, and joined with Great Britain to form the 'United Kingdom'. Ireland's MPs now sat in the Westminster Parliament. According to laws dating back to the seventeenth century, Catholics were unable to become Members of Parliament. This barrier was especially resented in Ireland where three-quarters of the population were Catholic.

In 1823 a Dublin lawyer, Daniel O'Connell, founded the Catholic Association. Its aim was to force the government to grant Catholic emancipation, giving Catholics the freedom to sit in Parliament. In 1828 O'Connell himself stood for election in County Clare against a popular Tory landowner, W. Vesey Fitzgerald:

Fellow Countrymen,
Your county wants a representative...
Of my qualification to fill that station, I leave you to judge. The habits of public speaking and many, many years of public business, render me, perhaps equally suited with most men to attend to the interests of Ireland in Parliament.
You will be told I am not qualified to be elected: the assertion, my friends, is untrue. I am qualified to be elected, and to be your representative. It is true that as a Catholic, I cannot, and of course never will, take the oaths at present prescribed to members of Parliament; but...I entertain a confident

hope that if you elect me, the most bigotted of our enemies will see the necessity of removing from the chosen representative of the people, an obstacle from doing his duty to his King and to his country.

(Daniel O'Connell's Election Address; in R. Huish, *Memoirs of Daniel O'Connell*, p. 438)

O'Connell won the election easily, but, as the law stood, he could not take his seat in Parliament. Most Tories were confident that the Prime Minister, the Duke of Wellington, and his Home Secretary, Sir Robert Peel, were men who could be relied on to resist the Catholic demands; but both were aware of the danger of sticking to this policy:

I have opposed what is called Catholic Emancipation. . . . But whatever may be my opinion upon these points, I cannot deny that the state of Ireland under existing circumstances is most unsatisfactory.

(Sir Robert Peel in August 1828; in C.S. Parker, *Sir Robert Peel*, vol. II, p. 55)

Faced, then, with the threat of open rebellion in Ireland if O'Connell did not take his seat, Wellington and Peel persuaded their colleagues (and the reluctant King George IV) to pass the Catholic Relief Act:

. . . from and after the commencement of this Act it shall be lawful for any person professing the Roman Catholic Religion to sit and vote in either House of Parliament, being in all other respects duly qualified . . .

(Public General Statutes, 1829; in Gash, *The Age of Peel*, p. 29)

The Act also opened nearly all official positions to Catholics.

QUESTIONS

1 *Why do you think there was little opposition to the repeal of the Test and Corporation Acts?*
2 *What did O'Connell hope to achieve, if he were victorious in the County Clare election?*
3 *What qualities did he possess, which made him suitable as a candidate?*
4 *How did O'Connell's victory place Wellington and Peel in a difficult position?*
5 *What do you think some Tories thought of this change of mind by their leaders? What effect would this have on the Tory party?*

The Old Parliamentary System

In Britain today all adults can vote. The only qualification for the *franchise* (right
to vote) is that the person should be over 18 years of age.

The parliamentary system of the early nineteenth century was very different. In
the first place, there were many different qualifications for the vote, varying from
place to place. One result of such qualifications was that the number of people
who could vote was very small – less than half a million in 1831, out of a population of 24 million.

Secondly, there were two different types of *constituency* (the area an MP rep-
resents). These were the *counties* and the *boroughs* (spelt 'burgh' in Scotland). In
England each county and borough, no matter their size, had two MPs; in Scotland
MPs were shared, although most counties did have one each. People complained
that, as the size of constituencies varied greatly, MPs were not shared evenly
throughout the country.

Thirdly, there was no secret ballot at this time – voting was done completely
openly. People complained that, as a result, elections could not possibly be fair.

In the early nineteenth century, then, the reformers wanted an extension of the
franchise, so that more people could vote; a fairer distribution of MPs; and fair
elections. We shall look at each of these demands in turn.

The franchise

... the members for the 52 counties are all elected by one uniform right.
Every man throughout England, possessed of 40 shillings per annum
freehold [land] ... is entitled to a vote ...

With respect to the different cities, towns, and boroughs, they exercise
a variety of separate and distinct rights ... In the greater part of them indeed
the right of voting appears to be vested in the freemen of bodies corporate,
but, under this general description, an infinite diversity of peculiar customs
is to be found. In some places the number of voters is limited to a select
body not exceeding 30 or 40; in others it is extended to 8, or 10 000. In
some places the freeman must be a resident inhabitant to entitle him to a
vote; in others his presence is only required at an election ...

The remaining rights of voting are of a still more complicated description.
Burgageholds [occupancy of a certain house], leaseholds, and freeholds, –
scot and lot [men who paid these ancient taxes], inhabitants householders,
inhabitants at large, potwallopers [owners of a hearth big enough to boil a

pot], and commonalty, each in different boroughs prevail, and create endless misunderstandings . . .

(*Report of the Society of the Friends of the People*, 9 February 1793)

Glasgow's number of inhabitants exceeds 77 000; its delegate is chosen by thirty-two members of the town council, who are all self-elected; and this delegate has only one voice of four in the choice of a member of Parliament with the delegates of three little towns [Dumbarton, Renfrew and Rutherglen].

Of fifteen members for the cities and burghs, one for Edinburgh is chosen by thirty-three persons; the other fourteen by sixty-five delegates, who are elected by 1220 persons.

The inhabitants of Scotland are above two million; their representatives are chosen by 3844.

(T.H.B. Oldfield, *The Representative History of Great Britain and Ireland*, vol. VI, p. 190–3)

Many boroughs had fewer voters than Glasgow or Edinburgh; for example, Sir Philip Francis gave an account of his election at Appleby in 1802:

The Fact is that yesterday morning between 11 & 12 I was unanimously elected by one Elector, to represent this Ancient Borough in Parliament . . . There was no other Candidate, no Opposition, no Poll demanded, Scrutiny, or petition. So I had nothing to do but thank the said Elector for the Unanimous Voice by which I was chosen. On Friday Morning I shall quit this Triumphant Scene with flying Colours, and a noble Determination not to see it again in less than seven years.

(*Francis Letters*, vol. II, p. 493; in Julius West, *A History of the Chartist Movement*, p. 14)

QUESTIONS

1 *State the qualification for the vote in the counties.*
2 *(a) The counties had a single qualification; how were the boroughs different?*
   (b) Give examples of some of the different borough qualifications under these headings: (i) freeman boroughs (ii) corporation boroughs, such as Glasgow (iii) burgage boroughs (iv) 'scot and lot' boroughs (v) potwalloper boroughs (vi) 'pocket boroughs', such as Appleby?.
3 *Write down your comments on the number of people who could vote, using all the information given.*

The Old Parliamentary System

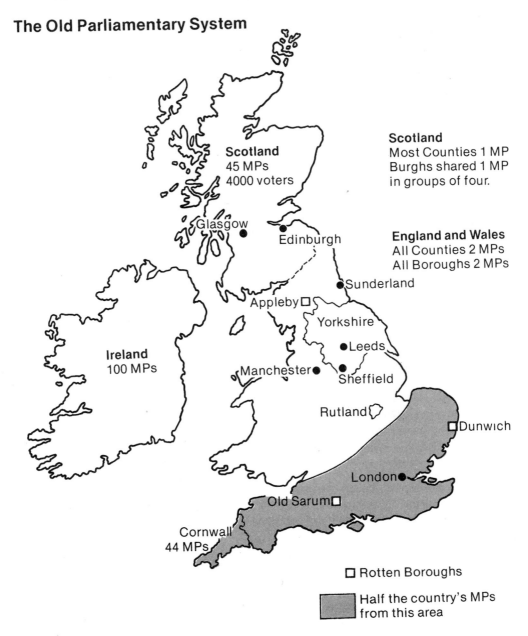

Scotland
45 MPs
4000 voters

Scotland
Most Counties 1 MP
Burghs shared 1 MP
in groups of four.

Glasgow
Edinburgh

England and Wales
All Counties 2 MPs
All Boroughs 2 MPs

Sunderland
Appleby

Yorkshire

Ireland
100 MPs

Leeds

Manchester
Sheffield

Rutland

Dunwich

London

Old Sarum

Cornwall
44 MPs

☐ Rotten Boroughs

Half the country's MPs
from this area

The Constituencies

Nowadays, an attempt is made to make constituencies as nearly equal in population as possible, so that everybody is represented by an MP on an equal basis. This was not the case in the early nineteenth century. (See map opposite.)

> A stranger . . . would be very much astonished if he were taken to a ruined mound, and told that that mound sent two representatives to Parliament – if he were taken to a stone wall and told that three niches in it sent two representatives to Parliament – if he were taken to a park, where no houses were to be seen, and told that that park sent two representatives; but if he were told this and were astonished at hearing it, he would be still more astonished if he were to see large and opulent towns full of enterprise and industry, and intelligence, containing vast magazines of every species of manufactures, and were told that these towns sent no representatives to Parliament.
> (Speech in the House of Lords by Lord John Russell, 1831)

> The county of Yorkshire, which contains nearly a million of souls, sends two county members; and so does Rutland, which contains not an hundredth part of that number. The town of Old Sarum, which contains not three houses, sends two members; and the town of Manchester, which contains upwards of sixty thousand souls, is not admitted to send any. Is there any principle in these things?
> (Thomas Paine, *Rights of Man*, 1791)

> Old Sarum is an area about one hundred yards in diameter taking in the whole crown of a hill. Near this is one farm house, which is all that remains of any town in or near the place, for the encampment has no resemblance of a town; and yet this is called the borough of Old Sarum, and sends two members to Parliament; who these members can justly say they represent, would be hard for them to answer.
> (Daniel Defoe, *A Tour through the Whole Island of Great Britain*, 1726)

QUESTIONS

1 (a) *How many MPs did each county and borough in England have?*
   (b) *The map shows that Cornwall had 44 MPs. How many boroughs were there in Cornwall? Explain your answer.*
2 (a) *Which parts of the country had: (i) too many MPs, (ii) too few MPs?*

(b) *What great change, dealt with in Chapter 1, had helped to produce this unfair distribution of MPs?*

3   *Old Sarum was one of many 'rotten' boroughs. Describe Old Sarum, and explain why the term 'rotten' borough was appropriate.*

4   *Do you think Manchester was fairly represented?*

Elections

Only landowners could stand for Parliament. Many seats were controlled by one family, so a choice of candidates was very rare. Where elections did take place, they were dominated by bribery and corruption. The main reason for this was that there was no secret ballot – a voter had to climb on to a special platform known as the hustings and announce to the crowd the name of the candidate for whom he was voting. This obviously opened the door to widespread unfairness. A writer in *The Extraordinary Blue Book* – one of many radical pamphlets and newspapers of the time – gave examples:

> At Nottingham, one gentleman confessed to having paid away in the election of 1826, above £3000 in bribery in a single day. At Leicester, the voters, in anticipation of a contest, expressed their hope that the price of votes might rise to £10, as they said it commonly did, if the struggle was severe. At Hull, one of the sitting members dared not appear before his constituents – not for any defalcation [fault] of duty in Parliament, but because he had not paid 'the polling money' for the last election.
> (The Extraordinary Blue Book, 1831)

> Some seats are private property; the right of voting belongs to a few house-holders . . . and . . . these votes are commanded by the owner of the estate. The fewer they are, the more easily they are managed . . . Where the number of voters is greater, . . . the business is more difficult and . . . expensive. The candidate . . . must deal individually with the constituents, who sell themselves to the highest bidder . . . At Aylesbury a bowl of guineas stood in the committee-room, and the voters were helped out of it. The price of votes varies according to their number. In some places it is as low as forty shillings, in others . . . it is thirty pounds.
> (Robert Southey, *Letters from England*, 1807)

Bribery was not the only way of securing votes, as a Parliamentary Committee heard:

Show of Hands for a Liberal Candidate.

971. Have you ever known intimidation practiced to any extent at a county election? – Yes, by landlords over tenants.

972. In what ways have they exercised that intimidation? – By insisting upon their voting as the landlord wished, and it was perfectly understood by them that they would lose their farms if they voted contrary to the wishes and inclinations of their landlords . . .

(Report of the Select Committee on Bribery at Elections, *Parliamentary Papers*, 1835, viii, p. 58–9)

Charles Dickens used his novels to show up some of the defects of the Parliamentary system. This is part of a description of an election as seen through the eyes of Mr. Pickwick:

During the whole time of the polling, the town was in a perpetual fever of excitement. Exciseable articles were remarkably cheap at all the public houses; and spring vans paraded the streets for the accommodation of voters who were seized with any temporary dizziness in the head – an epidemic which prevailed among the electors, during the contest, to a most alarming extent, and under the influence of which they might frequently be seen lying on the pavements in a state of utter insensibility. A small body of electors remained unpolled on the very last day. They were calculating and reflecting persons, who had not yet been convinced by the arguments of either party, although they had had frequent conferences with each. One hour before the close of the poll, Mr. Perker [Slumkey's agent] solicited the honour of a private interview with these intelligent, these noble, these patriotic men. It was granted. His arguments were brief, but satisfactory. They went in a body to the poll; and when they returned, the honourable Samuel Slumkey, of Slumkey Hall, was returned also.

(Charles Dickens, *The Posthumous Papers of the Pickwick Club*, 1901 edition, pp. 136–7)

QUESTIONS

1 *Describe the way in which an elector actually voted, and explain why this made cheating easy.*
2 *List the different ways in which candidates attempted to ensure support, as shown in the extracts and cartoon.*
3 *Why did the price paid for votes rise higher at some elections than at others?*
4 (a) *What do you think caused the epidemic of 'temporary dizziness in the head' among the electors described by Charles Dickens?*
   (b) *What form do you think the 'brief, but satisfactory' arguments of Mr. Perker took?*

Arguments over Reform

The old Parliamentary system was thus grossly unfair and corrupt, and worked almost entirely for the benefit of one group, the landowners. Demands for change came from the working class, whose spokesmen were Radicals like Henry 'Orator' Hunt and William Cobbett, and from the middle classes:

> It will be asked, will a reform of Parliament give the labouring man a cow or a pig; will it put bread and cheese into his satchel instead of infernal cold potatoes; will it give him a bottle of beer to carry to the field instead of making him lie down on his belly to drink out of the brook . . .? Will Parliamentary Reform put an end to the harnessing of men and women by a

hired overseer to draw carts like beasts of burden; will it put an end to the system which causes the honest labourer to be worse fed than the felons in the jails? . . . The enemies of reform jeeringly ask us, whether reform would do these things for us; and I answer distinctly THAT IT WOULD DO THEM ALL.
(William Cobbett, *Political Register*, 1832)

In Birmingham in 1830, Thomas Attwood, a middle-class banker, formed the Birmingham Political Union to press for reform. The Union was important as it attempted to unite different groups behind the demand. Soon, Political Unions sprang up in other towns as well:

That honourable House [of Commons], in its present state, is evidently too far removed in habits, wealth and station, from the wants and interests of the lower and middle classes of the people, to have . . . any close identity of feeling with them. The great aristocratical interests of all kinds are well represented there . . . But the interests of Industry and of Trade have scarcely any representatives at all!
(*Declaration of the Birmingham Political Union*, 1830, p. 7)

Some Whigs were also in favour of political reform. Although they were land-owners like the Tories, they were worried about the possibility of revolution in Britain. Two things made this fear very real in 1830. In the south of England, bad harvests and extreme poverty had led to outbreaks of violence among agricultural labourers. This violence, supposedly led by a mysterious figure called 'Captain Swing' was later referred to as 'the last labourers' revolt'. In the summer of 1830, more worrying news was heard – the French king had been overthrown by a revolution led by the middle classes. A rising young politician, T.B. Macaulay, put the fears felt by these Whigs into words:

At present we oppose the schemes of revolutionaries . . . Yet, saying this, we exclude great masses of property and intelligence from Parliament . . . We do more. We drive over to the side of revolution those whom we shut out from power.
(T.B. Macaulay, Speech in the House of Commons, 2 March 1831)

Most Tories were against reform. The existing system suited them well enough, since it served their landowning interests. Many Tories actually believed that no other class of person could be fit to take part in government.

The "System" that "Works so Well"!! or The Boroughmongers GRINDING machine.

In 1830 the Tory Prime Minister, the Duke of Wellington, gave his view on reform to the House of Lords:

> I, on my own part, will go further, and say, that I never read or heard of any measure . . . which in any degree satisfies my mind that the state of representation can be improved . . . I will go further and say, that the Legislature [Parliament] and the system of representation possesses the full and entire confidence of the country . . . Under these circumstances, I am not prepared to bring forward any measure of reform . . . I shall always feel it my duty to resist such measures when proposed by others . . .
> (Duke of Wellington, Speech in House of Lords, 2 November 1830)

That statement by the Duke of Wellington sealed the fate of his government.

The Tories were already badly split, following Catholic Emancipation, and had only just remained in power after the election of 1830; now they were defeated in a vote in the House of Commons and were forced to resign. King William IV asked the Whig leader Earl Grey to form a new government. The Whigs had called for Parliamentary reform during the election campaign in 1830, so the country waited expectantly for a reform bill.

The Time-table of Reform

Nov. 1830–   Tory government fell from power; Whigs formed government.

Mar. 1831–   Lord John Russell presented a reform bill to the House of Commons, but the bill was defeated, so the government resigned.

May 1831–   General Election – Whigs returned with increased majority.

Oct. 1831–   Second attempt at Reform defeated by House of Lords. The country erupted in fury, with riots in Bristol, Derby and Nottingham.

May 1832–   Third Reform Bill interfered with by Lords. Grey now asked the King to create 50 new Whig peers (members of the House of Lords) in order to swamp the Tory majority there. The King would only permit 20, so government resigned.

The 'May   The King now asked the Duke of Wellington to form a govern-
Days'–   ment. This led to renewed riots and protests throughout the country. The Birmingham Political Union announced that 200 000 men would march on London and stay there until reform was passed. People put up signs saying: 'No taxes paid here till the Reform Bill is passed'. Francis Place urged people: 'To Stop the Duke Go For Gold' – he hoped that if enough people withdrew their money from the banks there would be a financial crisis. Faced with this widespread opposition, Wellington informed the King that he was unable to form a government.

May 1832–   Grey returned as Prime Minister, armed with a promise from the king to create new Whig peers if necessary, but Wellington now urged his party not to oppose the bill.

June 1832–   The Reform Act became law.

The Reform Act

The Act brought about two main changes, affecting the franchise and the distribution of parliamentary seats.

The franchise

In the *counties*, two new groups of voters joined the 40*s*. freeholders – the £10 copyholders (an old form of lease); and the £50 lease-holders.

The greatest change affected the *borough* franchise, where, as we have seen, a great number of qualifications existed:

> . . . in every City or Borough which shall return a Member or Members to serve in any future Parliament, every Male Person of full Age, and not subject to any legal Incapacity, who shall occupy . . . as Owner or Tenant, any House, Warehouse, Counting-House, Shop, or other Building, ... of the clear yearly Value of not less than Ten Pounds shall . . . be entitled to vote in the Election of a Member or Members to serve in any future Parliament for such City or Borough . . .
> (The Reform Act, 7 June 1832; in Gash, *Age of Peel*, p. 48)

Thus a single uniform qualification had been created in the boroughs, entitling the £10 householders to vote.

The distribution of seats

56 of the most 'rotten boroughs' (including Old Sarum, Appleby and Dunwich) lost both their MPs; 30 slightly less rotten boroughs lost one MP. With other small changes, this provided 145 seats to be redistributed.

These were given to the counties and cities of the north, so that for the first time towns such as Manchester, Sunderland, Leeds and Sheffield would have their own representatives in Parliament. Eight seats were given to the Scottish burghs, bringing Scotland's representation up to 53; five more seats were given to Ireland.

QUESTIONS

1   Explain briefly in your own words how William Cobbett believed a reform of Parliament could benefit working people.

2   Why did Attwood and the Birmingham Political Union want reform?

3   Why had some Whigs come round to support reform?

4   What was the Duke of Wellington's attitude to reform? Why do you think he had this view?

5   During the struggle to pass the Reform bill, why did Grey, the Whig leader, ask the King to create more Whig peers?

6   Briefly summarise the terms of the Reform Act.

Effects of reform

A month after the 1832 Reform Act was passed, William Cobbett wrote:

> Every sensible man sees that the Reform Bill is the commencement of a mighty revolution.
> (Cobbett, *Political Register*, 7 July 1832)

The Act was very important in the following ways:
For the first time, the middle class had the vote. Industrial and commercial interests could thus be represented.

> ...power is transferred from one class of society, the gentlemen of England, to another class of society, the shopkeepers.
> (Duke of Wellington; in L.J. Jennings (ed.), *The Croker Papers*)

The middle class brought new ideas to Parliament, which now started on a programme of important reforms (see Chapters 5 and 6). The movement towards Free Trade and the Repeal of the Corn Laws in the 1840s (dealt with in Chapter 8), shows the growing influence of the middle class over the old aristocracy. The Reform Act of 1832 marked a new beginning. The parliamentary system had been unchanged for centuries; the 1832 Act paved the way for further change. Half a century later, nearly all men could vote; within a century, women also had the right to vote and to stand for parliament.
  The 1832 Reform Act did mark an important new beginning, but the Act itself left many areas where further reform was needed.

The increase in the size of the electorate was small – from about 480 000 to 814 000 over the country as a whole – only one man in six had the vote.

Landowners still dominated political affairs, as Wellington noticed:

> I don't think that the influence of property in this country is diminished. That is to say that the gentry have as many followers, and influence as many voters at elections as they ever did.
> (Duke of Wellington; in Jennings (ed.), *Croker Papers*)

The distribution of seats was still unfair. The south of England was still overrepresented at the expense of the industrial areas, while some 'rotten' and 'pocket' boroughs still existed.

There was no change in the system of voting, so bribery and corruption continued at elections as before, as the new voters soon found out.

> Intimidation is practiced in towns by the threat of taking away your own custom, and by inducing others, over whom you have influence, to take away theirs, too, and by a general threat of doing all the injury to the tradesmen within the range of your power.
> ('Report of the Select Committee on Bribery at Elections', *Parliamentary Papers*, 1835, viii, p. 59)

> Principle [honesty] is unknown among the electors, the far greater proportion of whom are free burgesses of the lowest order, and require feasting and treating and other weighty considerations to bring them to the poll.
> (*Morning Chronicle*, 7 January 1835)

The working class were bitterly disappointed by the Act.

> When the Bill is safe, we cannot think so ill of human nature as to think that those who will have gained their freedom, will not aid us to gain ours.
> (*Poor Man's Guardian*, 26 May 1832)

Just six months later, the same writer was expressing his doubts:

> We have often told you the Reform Bill would do you no good . . . The great majority of the new electors are middlemen who thrive by your degradation . . .
> (*Poor Man's Guardian*, 15 December 1832)

> Fellow Countrymen,
> It is now nearly six years since the Reform Bill became a part of the laws of our country. To carry that measure . . . the co-operation of the millions was sought for and cheerfully and honestly given. . . . Alas, their hopes were excited by promises which have not been kept, and their expectations of freedom have been bitterly disappointed in seeing the men, whom they had assisted to power, spurning their petition with contempt, and binding them down by still more slavish enactments . . .
> (William Lovett, *Life and Struggles*, 1876 p. 118–9)

William Lovett was one of the founders of the Chartist movement, which aimed to get working-class people into Parliament. Disappointment with the Reform Act was one of the major reasons for its development (see Chapter 7).

QUESTIONS

1 (a) *In what way did the Reform Act mark a beginning?*
   (b) *Who were the new class to get the vote? How did they prove important?*
2 (a) *List four areas in which further reform was needed.*
   (b) *Explain how land owners could still dominate political affairs.*

ASSIGNMENTS

A. *'Preparing the way'. Show how the Repeal of the Test and Corporations Acts and Catholic Emancipation were important in preparing the way for the Reform Act.*
B. *Draw up a list of ways in which the old parliamentary system was different from our system of today.*
C. *Study the Cruikshank cartoon on page 55, and then write a short essay explaining all the defects of the Parliamentary system shown there.*
D. *Write down the groups who (a) favoured reform, (b) opposed reform, and explain why they held these views.*
E. *Imagine you lived at the time of the passing of the first Reform Act, and kept a diary of the main events. Write down some extracts from your diary dealing with the events of 1830–32, showing the struggle to pass the Bill.*
F. *'A mighty revolution'. How far do you think the Reform Bill justified Cobbett's description?*

5 Working in Factories and Mines

Working in the Factories

In 1815, the factory system in the textile industry was rapidly replacing the old domestic system, especially in the manufacture of cotton (see Chapter 1, pages 8–11). At first the government did little to control factory working conditions. It was therefore up to each individual mill-owner how he treated his employees. In many cases, this led to dreadful working conditions for the men, women and young children who laboured in the mills.

Peter Gaskell described a fairly typical day in the life of a factory worker in 1833:

> Rising at or before day-break, between four and five o'clock the year round ... he swallows a hasty meal, or hurries to the mill without taking any food whatever. At eight o'clock half an hour, and in some instances forty minutes, are allowed for breakfast. In many cases, the engine continues at work during mealtime, obliging the labourer to eat and still overlook his work ...
>
> ... After this, he is incessantly engaged – not a single minute of rest or relaxation being allowed him.
>
> At twelve o'clock, the engine stops, and an hour is given for dinner ...
>
> ... As soon as this is effected, the family is again scattered. No rest has been taken; ...
>
> Again they are closely immured [i.e. confined to the mill] from one o'clock till eight or nine, with the exception of twenty minutes, this being allowed for tea, or baggin-time, as it is called. This imperfect meal is almost universally taken in the mill: ... During the whole of this long period, they are actively and unremittingly engaged in a crowded room and an elevated

temperature, so that, when finally dismissed for the day, they are exhausted equally in body and mind.
(Peter Gaskell, *The Manufacturing Population of England*, 1833, Chapters 4 and 5)

The temperature and atmosphere commonly found in textile factories was described by William Cobbett in his *Political Register*:

> ... In the cotton-spinning work, these creatures are kept ... in a heat of from eighty to eighty-four degrees.
> ... The door of the place wherein they work, *is locked, except half an hour*, at tea-time, the work people are not allowed to send for water to drink, in the hot factory;
> ... In addition, there are the dust, and what is called cotton-flyings or fuz, which the unfortunate creatures have to inhale; and the fact is, ... that well constitutioned men are rendered old and past labour at forty years of age, and the children are rendered decrepit and deformed.
> (Cobbett, *Political Register*, vol. LII, 20 November 1824)

Unguarded machinery led to many serious accidents:

> The accidents which occur to the manufacturing population of Birmingham are very severe and numerous ... Many are the consequences of the want of proper attention to the fencing of machinery, which appears to be seldom thought of ... : and many are caused by loose portions of dress being caught by the machinery, so as to drag the unfortunate sufferers under its power. The shawls of the females, or their long hair, and the aprons and loose sleeves of the boys and men, are in this way frequent causes of dreadful multilation.
> ('Report on the Sanitary Condition of the Labouring Population'; *Parliamentary Papers*, 1842, vol. 27, p. 208)

Most factory owners had strict rules for their workers:

> ... In some mills, the crime of sitting down to take a little rest is visited with a penalty of *one shilling*, [5p], but let the masters and their rules speak for themselves.
> 1st. The door of the lodge will be closed ten minutes after the engine starts every morning, and no weaver will afterwards be admitted till

breakfast-time. Any weaver who shall be absent during that time shall forfeit three-pence [1p] per loom . . .

   9th. All shuttles, brushes, oil cans, wheels, windows etc. if broken, shall be paid for by the weaver.

   11th. If any hand in the mill is seen *talking* to another, *whistling*, or *singing*, will be fined sixpence [2½p].

   16th. . . . Any weaver seen from his work during mill hours, will be fined *sixpence*.

(James Leach, *Stubborn Facts from the Factories by a Manchester Operative*, published and dedicated to the working classes by William Rathleigh, M.P., 1844, pp. 11–15)

QUESTIONS

1   (a) How long was the working day of the factory workers, according to the first extract? How does this compare with the average length of the working day today?

(b) What complaints could be made about the meal breaks?

(c) In what ways would a factory worker's life be restricted, because of the long working hours?

2   In what ways was mill working: (a) dangerous to health?

(b) harsh and unpleasant?

3   Why do you think the factory owners had such strict rules?

The mill children

These appalling conditions applied to most factory workers, but young children were particularly at risk:

   Elizabeth Bentley, age 23, lives at Leeds, began work at the age of six in Mr. Busk's flax-mill . . . Hours 5 a.m. till 9 p.m. when they were 'thronged', otherwise 6 a.m. to 7 at night, with 40 minutes for meal at noon.

   . . . Does that keep you constantly on your feet? – Yes, there are so many frames, and they run so quick. Your labour is very excessive? – Yes; you have not time for anything. Suppose you flagged a little, or were too late, what would they do? – Strap us. Girls as well as boys? – Yes. Have you ever been strapped? – Yes. Severely? – Yes.

   Were the girls so struck as to leave marks upon their skin? – Yes, they

Factory Inspector at Work   *Mill Children*

have had black marks many a time, and their parents dare not come to him about it, they are afraid of losing their work.
(Committee on Factory Children's Labour, *Parliamentary Papers*, 1831–2, vol. XV, pp. 195–99)

Such working conditions had an inevitable effect on children:

I have seen them fall asleep, and they have been performing their work with their hands while they were asleep . . . when their work was over.
(Evidence given by Joseph Badder, a spinner at Mr. Bradley's, Leicester, and collected by Mr. Drinkwater; Factory Commission, 1833; *Parliamentary Papers* vol. XX, page Ci, 19)

Many a time has been so fatigued that she could hardly take off her clothes at night, or put them on in the morning; her mother would be raging at her, because when she sat down she could not get up again.
(*Parliamentary Papers*, 1833, vol. XX, pp. 25–7)

Pauper apprentices

One group of children was even worse off than the rest, if that is possible to imagine. These were the pauper apprentices. They were children in the care of the local parish, who had the right to bind them as apprentices to mill-owners, usually until the children had reached the age of twenty-one. They were supposed to be learning a trade, but were more often given only unskilled work, and were frequently unpaid during their apprenticeship.

A Report in 1816 on children working in factories produced this evidence about pauper apprentices:

> Were any children employed in those mills? – There were 111 children employed when I went there at first, and as many as 150 when I left. All parish apprentices, chiefly from London – the parishes of Whitechapel, St. James' and St. Clement's, I think. There was a few from Liverpool workhouse. Those that came from London were from seven to eleven; those from Liverpool were from eight or ten to fifteen . . .
>
> What were the hours of work? – From 5 o'clock in the morning till eight at night all the year through. What time was allowed for meals? – Half an hour for breakfast and half an hour for dinner.
>
> (Evidence given by Mr. John Moss, master of the apprentices, in charge of the apprentice house at Backbarrow, from the 'Report on the Children employed in Manufactories; *Parliamentary Papers*, 1816, vol. III, pp. 178– 185)

Robert Blincoe, an orphan boy, told of his first arrival at the apprentice-house beside the factory in which he was to work:

> . . . when he . . . was told that it was to be his home for 14 years to come, he was not greatly delighted, so closely did it resemble a workhouse. When the first cart, in which was young Blincoe, drove up to the door, a number of villagers flocked round, some of whom exclaimed, 'God help the poor little wretches!' 'Eh!' said another, 'what a fine collection of children, little do they know to what a life of slavery they are doomed'. 'The Lord have mercy on them', said a third. 'They'll find little mercy here', said a fourth.
>
> (John Brown, *A Memoir of Robert Blincoe, an Orphan Boy*, . . . Manchester, 1832)

QUESTIONS

1   *At what age did Elizabeth Bentley begin mill work?*
2   (*a*) *Why was it necessary to beat the children?*
    (*b*) *Why were there few complaints at this treatment?*

(*c*) *What would have been a more sensible solution to the tiredness of the children?*

3 *'... her mother would be raging at her.' How can you explain the mother's insistence that the child go to work?*

4 *Apart from the working conditions which affected all children in the factories, what added misery was there in the life of a pauper apprentice?*

5 *Which of the two illustrations of factory children (page 67) do you consider to be the most accurate, and why?*

Exceptions to the rule

Not all factory owners were cruel or unsympathetic towards their employees. Some employers owned what were, for their time, model factories. Perhaps the best known of these men was Robert Owen. In 1799 Owen became the proprietor of the New Lanark Mills. These were situated below the Falls of Clyde, and had been established in 1786 by Owen's father-in-law, David Dale. By 1793, they had become the largest cotton spinning mills in Europe.

Here is how Robert Owen described conditions at New Lanark (shown above):

The system of receiving apprentices from public charities was abolished; permanent settlers with large families were encouraged, and comfortable houses built for their accommodation. The practice of employing children in the mills, of six, seven and eight years of age, was discontinued, and their parents advised to allow them to acquire health and education until they were ten years old ... The children were taught reading, writing and arithmetic during five years, that is, from five to ten, in the village school, without expense to their parents ...

... Their houses [i.e. the workers'] were rendered more comfortable, their streets were improved, the best provisions were purchased, and sold to them at low rates ... Fuel and clothes were obtained for them in the same manner ... Those employed became industrious, temperate, healthy, faithful to their employers, and kind to each other.
(Robert Owen, *A New View of Society*, 1831)

Deanston Cotton mill, near Doune, in Perthshire, enjoyed a similar reputation:

... [it] is one of these beautifully situated and admirably regulated great manufacturing establishments which it is a pleasure to see ... The apartments in the mill are, clean, well-ventilated, and have the machinery well fenced ... The general heat of the apartments is from 65° to 70° ...

There are here ... a pipe of water in each story; sewering arrangement is adopted throughout ...

... and a more cheerful, happy-looking set of industrious men and women, and of young people, is seldom, if I am not mistaken, to be found.
(James Stuart's reports on Scottish factories, *Parliamentary Papers*, 1833, vol. XX, p. 16)

QUESTIONS

1   (a) *Below what age were children not employed at New Lanark?*
    (b) *What reason did Robert Owen have for this?*
2   *Make a list of the ways in which working at New Lanark and Deanston must have been safer and more enjoyable than in most factories at the time.*
3   *What effect did these improved conditions have on the work force at New Lanark and Deanston?*

Factory Reform

The government and factory reform – To intervene or not to intervene?

The attitude of Parliament at the time to matters such as factory conditions was one of *laissez-faire*, that is, of non-intervention. However, factory conditions aroused bitter argument. Some people felt that the bad conditions in factories had been exaggerated, and that, in any case, long hours of work were essential to industry.

A prominent economist of the day, Nassau Senior, put forward this argument:

> 2d. The exceeding easiness of cotton-factory labour renders long hours of work practicable. With the exception of the mule spinners . . . the work is merely that of watching the machinery, and piecing the threads that break. I have seen the girls who thus attend standing with their arms folded during the whole time that I stayed in the room – others sewing a handkerchief or sitting down . . .
>
> Under these circumstances, factories have always worked for very long hours. From thirteen to fifteen, or even sixteen, appear to be the usual hours per day abroad . . . Any plan therefore, which should reduce the present comparatively short hours, must either destroy profit, or reduce wages to the Irish standard, or raise the price of the commodity.
>
> (Nassau Senior, *Letters on the Factory Act*, 1837)

QUESTIONS

1 *(a) Why did Senior insist that long hours did no physical harm to mill-workers?*
(b) Give one other reason why he said it was against workers' interests to shorten working hours.
2 *How would shorter working hours affect factory owners?*

The campaign for factory reform

There had been early Factory Acts, in 1802 (regulating the employment of pauper apprentices) and in 1819 (limiting the working hours of young children) but they had both been ineffective as there were no adequate means of enforcing them.

In the early 1830s, however, the campaign for government action to ensure a ten-hour working day for women and children got under way. (At the time, Parliament was opposed to limiting men's working hours, as it felt men should be free to arrange their own conditions of work.) The campaign featured such well-meaning factory owners as John Fielden and John Wood, and from 1830, the 'Ten Hours Movement' as it was known, was led by Richard Oastler, a Tory estate agent. Oastler made a series of emotional speeches, and wrote a letter to the *Leeds Mercury* which became famous:

Let truth speak out, appalling as the statement may appear. The fact is true. Thousands of our fellow creatures and fellow subjects, both male and female, the miserable inhabitants of a *Yorkshire town* . . . are at this very moment existing in a state of slavery, *more horrid* than are the victims of that hellish system *'colonial slavery'*! . . . The very streets which receive the droppings of an 'Anti-Slavery Society' are every morning wet by the tears of innocent victims at the accursed shrine of avarice, who are *compelled* (not by the cartwhip of the negro slave-driver) but by the dread of the equally appalling thong or strap of the over-looker, to hasten, half dressed, *but not half fed*, to those magazines of British infantile slavery – *the worsted mills in the town and neighbourhood of Bradford*!
(Richard Oastler, *Leeds Mercury*, October 16, 1830)

Oastler's friend, the Tory MP Michael Sadler, introduced a 'Ten Hours Bill' into Parliament in 1832, but this fell through when Sadler lost his seat after the first Parliamentary Reform Act of 1832. Parliamentary leadership of the campaign then passed to the Tory Lord Ashley (who became the Earl of Shaftesbury in 1851). In 1833 a Royal Commission reported on factory conditions. The Commission was very critical of the way in which many factories were being run and of conditions in them and its recommendations were included, and even improved upon, in Lord Althorp's Factory Act of 1833.

1833 Factory Act

. . . no person under eighteen years of age shall [work] between half past eight in the evening and half past five in the morning, in any cotton, woollen, worsted, hemp, flax, tow, linen or silk mill . . .

. . . no person under the age of eighteen shall be employed in any such mill . . . more than twelve hours in . . . one day, nor more than sixty-nine hours in . . . one week.

There shall be allowed . . . not less than one and a half hours for meals.

It shall not be lawful . . . to employ in any factory . . . as aforesaid, except in mills for the manufacture of silk, any child who shall not have completed his or her ninth year.

It shall not be lawful for any person to employ . . . in any factory . . . as aforesaid for longer than forty-eight hours in one week, nor for longer than nine hours in one day, any child who shall not have completed his or her eleventh year . . . or . . . twelfth year . . . or . . . thirteenth year.

> It shall be lawful for His Majesty to appoint four Inspectors of factories . . . empowered to enter any . . . mill, and any school . . . belonging thereto, at all times . . .
>
> Every child restricted to the performance of forty-eight hours of labour in any one week shall attend some school.
>
> (*Statutes of the Realm*, 3 & 4 William IV, c. 103)

The factory schools which were set up after the Factory Act of 1833 varied tremendously, as it was left to each individual factory owner to provide education for the children he employed. The place of education, for example, might be the factory 'coal–hole' or 'engine–house', as Inspector Saunders found to be the case in Yorkshire in 1838.

QUESTIONS

1   (a) *To whom did Richard Oastler compare the workers in the Bradford worsted mills?*
(b) *In what ways were the Bradford workers as badly off, or worse off, than these people?*
2   (a) *To which type of factories did the 1833 Factory Act apply?*
(b) *Who were forbidden to be employed in such factories?*
(c) *How were working hours restricted for children i) from 13 to 18 years ii) from 9 to 13 years?*
(d) *What did the Act say about meal-breaks?*
(e) *How was this Act to be enforced?*
3   *Consider the limitations of the Act:*
(a) *To whom did the terms of the Act not apply?*
(b) *How clear was the Act about the provision of education for children under 13 years old?*
(c) *Do you consider there was adequate provision for enforcement of the Act?*
(d) *Comment on the number of hours which could still be worked by children from 9 to 13 years, and from 13 to 18 years.*
(e) *There was no compulsory registration of births, marriages and deaths until 1836. How would this affect the working of the Act until then?*

1844 Factory Act

Ashley continued with the campaign for a ten-hour working day, and in 1844, after the report of a Parliamentary Committee, the government introduced a Bill which became the Factory Act of 1844. This Act limited women's working hours – for the first time – to twelve a day, but as a concession to factory owners, lowered the minimum age for children in textile factories from 9 to 8 years. However, these children were now only allowed to work six and a half hours a day, instead of the nine hours laid down in the 1833 Act. Robert Peel, now Prime Minister, opposed the introduction of a ten-hour working day, as he felt that British industry would then not be able to withstand foreign competition.

1847 The 'Ten Hours Act'

It was not until 1847 that John Fielden managed to persuade Parliament at last to pass the 'Ten Hours Act', limiting working hours for women and children to ten a day. Lord Ashley now addressed his supporters:

> We have won the great object of all our labours – the Ten Hours Bill has become the law of the land; and we may hope, nay, we believe, that we shall find in its happy results, a full compensation for all our toils . . .
> (Lord Ashley's letter to the Short Time Committees; in E. Hodder, *'The Life and Work of the Seventh Earl of Shaftesbury'*, 1892, p. 369)

1850 Factory Act

The 'Ten Hours Act' of 1847 still had not limited in any way the hours worked by men. It was generally felt in Parliament that to do so was to restrict the freedom of a man to arrange his own terms of work with his employer. This view was expressed by Samuel Smiles, a popular journalist and author of the time:

> Even the best institutions can give a man no active aid. Perhaps the utmost they can do is, to leave him *free* to develop himself and improve his individual condition . . . there is no power of law that can make the idle man industrious, the thriftless provident, or the drunken sober; though every individual can be each and all of these if he will, by the exercise of his own free powers of action and self-denial.
> (Samuel Smiles, *Self-Help*, 1859, pp. 1–2)

Ashley and others in the 'Ten Hours Movement' thought that if women and children were restricted to a ten-hour working day, men should not work longer than ten hours either. Many factory owners managed to avoid restricting men's working hours by introducing a 'relay' system, staggering working hours for women and children so that factories could be kept open far longer than ten hours a day. This forced many unprotected male workers to work much longer than ten hours in a day.

Ashley therefore kept up the struggle for a strict ten-hour day for all. In 1850, however, he accepted a compromise with the government, which resulted in the Factory Act of 1850. By this Act, a ten and a half hour working day was introduced for all, but women and children's working hours were not to be outside 6 am to 6 pm (2 pm on Saturdays). Unfortunately this meant many now had to work an extra half hour a day. Ashley had unwisely not consulted textile workers in arriving at this compromise, and they now rejected his leadership.

QUESTIONS

1 In what way were factory owners avoiding their duty under the terms of the 1833 Factory Act?
2 In what way was the 1844 Factory Act a new departure from the Act of 1833?
3 Why did Samuel Smiles maintain that the working hours of men should not be limited by Parliament?
4 'We have won the great object of all our labours'. Was Ashley correct? Give a reason for your answer.
5 Explain why many factory workers were dissatisfied with the 1850 Factory Act.

ASSIGNMENTS

A. Sum up the arguments for, and against, the need for Parliament to regulate factory working conditions.
B. Describe a typical day in the life of a factory boy or girl before 1833. Compare this with working conditions for such children in 1851. What improvements had taken place, and what improvements had still not been carried out by 1851?

Working in the Mines

The coal industry was long established in Britain, dating back to the fifteenth century, at least. In the early eighteenth century, most mines were only shallow pits, or cuttings in hillsides where a coal seam came near the surface.

In the late eighteenth century, however, the Industrial Revolution caused a great expansion in coal mining. More coal was needed to provide steam power, and for iron smelting. Larger deeper mines became necessary, but the deeper mines went, the greater became the dangers to the health and safety of the mine workers. Men, women and very young children were employed by the mine owners of the time; often the family worked as a team in cutting the coal and bringing it to the surface.

LETTING CHILDREN DOWN A COAL MINE

Descending into the mine was always a dangerous undertaking. At first, a crude, hand-operated windlass was used. This method was later replaced, first by a horse-gin, and then by a steam engine, both of which were more powerful and more reliable than the original method.

Underground occupations

In the mines, men and older boys usually worked as 'hewers', cutting the coal from the coal face, often in narrow tunnels, or 'rooms' which could be as little as 45 centimetres in height.

No. 3. George Reid, 16 years old, coal hewer:

I pick the coal at the wall-face, and seldom do other work; have done so for six years; the seam is 26 inches [66 cm] high, and when I pick I am obliged to twist myself up; the men who work on this seam lie on their broadsides.

... it is horrible sore work; none ever come up to meals. Pieces of bread are taken down; boys and girls sometimes drink the water below, ...

I should not care about the work if we had not so much of it; have often been hurt; was off idle a short bit ago, the pick having torn my flesh while ascending the shaft. ... Six of the family work with father below.
(Children's Employment Commission, *Report on the Collieries and Iron Works in the East of Scotland*, 1842, vol. ii, p. 436)

The roofs of these tunnels were at first supported by uncut pillars of coal left by the hewers as they went along, but this was both unsafe and wasteful, and was gradually replaced by the practice of using wooden pit-props.

Young boys and girls, sometimes only 4 or 5 years old, but more commonly from 8 or 9, were employed to haul tubs or truck-loads of coal along the tunnel from the coal-face to the bottom of the pit shaft, from where they could be transported to the surface. These young 'drawers' as they were known, were very often the children of the 'hewers' who cut the coal to fill their 'corves', or coal tubs. It was back-breaking work, requiring all the physical effort of which these unfortunate youngsters were capable; they were harnessed like animals to their burdens.

Drawer

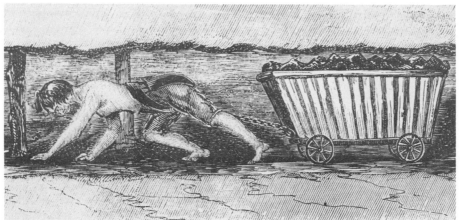

As the 'drawers' struggled along with their heavy loads, they passed a 'trapper' at intervals along the tunnel. 'Trappers' were young boys who sat in silence and darkness in a hole in the tunnel wall all day, waiting for a truck load of coal to come along, so that they could open a wooden ventilation door to let the 'drawers' pass with their loads and then close the door behind them.

> The children that excite the greatest pity are those who stand behind the doors to open and shut them: they are called trappers, who in the darkness, solitude and stillness as of night, eke out a miserable existence for the smallest of wages. I can never forget the first unfortunate creature that I met with: it was a boy of about eight years old, who looked at me as I passed with an expression the most abject and idiotic — like a thing, a creeping thing, peculiar to the place. On approaching and speaking to him he shrank trembling and frightened into a corner.
> (*Parliamentary Papers*, 1842, vol. XV, p. 72)

Trapper

Women were commonly employed as 'bearers', that is, they carried the coal from the bottom of the pit shaft to the surface, up a series of steep ladders. Harnessed to their backs were creels, or baskets, for the coal, and as much as 75 kg might be carried. As the illustration opposite shows, this was not only dangerous to the bearer herself, but also for the one behind her.

In 1842, Janet Cumming, a bearer in the East of Scotland described her work:

> No. 1 Janet Cumming, 11 years old, bears coals:
> Works with father; has done so for two years. Father gangs at two in the

morning; I gang with the women at five, and come up at five at night; work all night on Fridays, and come away at twelve in the day.

I carry the large bits of coal from the wall-face to the pit bottom, and the small pieces called chows, in a creel; the weight is usually a hundred weight ... it is some work to carry; it takes three journies to fill a tub of 4 cwt [200 kg] ... The roof is very low; I have to bend my back and legs, and the water comes frequently up to the calves of my legs; has no liking for the work; father makes me like it.

(Children's Employment Commission, *Report on the Collieries and Iron Works in the East of Scotland*, 1842, vol. ii p. 436)

By 1842, however, horse-gins, and in some places steam engines were used to haul coal to the surface, and in some areas such as the west of Scotland and the Tyne and Wear area in north-east England, it was not the usual practice to employ women underground at all.

Safety and health

As mines were dug deeper to satisfy the increasing demand for coal, the safety of the miners was put at greater risk. Roofs of tunnels collapsed through insufficient support. Flooding was always a problem in mines. Newcomen had invented a steam pumping engine in the early eighteenth century to prevent flooding, but it was expensive, and in many areas, particularly in Scotland, mine owners tended not to use it as the output of coal from their mines was insufficient to justify the expense. A more efficient steam engine was produced by James Watt, a native of Greenock (see chapter 1 page 10) and Matthew Boulton, a Birmingham businessman, and was first installed with great success in Bloomfield Colliery, near Dudley.

On Friday last, a Steam Engine constructed by Mr Watt's new Principles was set to work at Bloomfield Colliery, near Dudley in the Presence of its Proprietors . . .

From the first Movement of its setting to work, it emptied the Engine Pit (which is about 90 feet [27.5 m] deep and stood 57 feet [17.4 m] high in water) in less than an hour . . . it is capable of doing to a depth of 300 feet [91.4 m], or even 360 if wanted, with one Fourth of the Fuel that a common Engine would require to produce the same Quantity of Power.

(*Birmingham Gazette*, 11 March 1776)

The use of a steam pumping engine to prevent flooding allowed mines to be dug deeper. However, this increased the danger from poisonous and explosive gases, the most common of which was 'fire-damp' or methane gas, although this was rare in Scottish mines.

Mines were ventilated by having several shafts cut, and sometimes a fire was lit at the bottom of a shaft to cause hot air to rise and draw in cold, fresh air in its place. The trouble with this was, of course, that explosions could occur if gases came into contact with the fire. In 1815, both George Stephenson and Humphrey Davy invented safety lamps which cut down the risk of an explosion by protecting the miners' formerly naked flame. The Davy Lamp, with its wire-gauze protection, had the added advantage of its flame turning blue when gas was present.

However, mine disasters still occurred. As late as 1866, there was a tremendous explosion at Oaks Colliery, Barnsley, on 12 December of that year, killing about 350 people.

In their famous Report of 1842 into conditions in the mines, the Commissioners pointed out these, and other, causes of accidents:

19. That in all coal-fields, accidents of a fearful nature are extremely frequent . . .
20. That one of the most frequent causes of accidents in these mines is the want of superintendence by overlookers or otherwise to see to the security of machinery for letting down and bringing up the workpeople, the restriction of the number of persons who ascend or descend at a time, the state of the mine as to the quantity of noxious gas in it, the efficiency of the ventilation, the exactness with which the air-door keepers perform their duty, the places into which it is safe or unsafe to go with a naked lighted candle, and the security of the proppings to uphold the roof, etc.
23. That there are moreover two practices peculiar to a few districts which

deserve the highest reprobration, namely, – first, the practice not unknown in some of the smaller mines in Yorkshire, and common in Lancashire, of employing ropes that are unsafe for letting down and drawing up the work-people; and second, the practice, occasionally met with in Yorkshire, and common in Derbyshire and Lancashire, of employing boys at the steam engines for letting down and drawing up the workpeople.
(Children's Employment Commission (Mines), *Parliamentary Papers*, 1842, vol. XV, pp. 257–8)

Not surprisingly, many miners lost their lives in accidents, but the filthy conditions and harsh physical work in cramped surroundings also took their toll on miners' health. Coal-dust was everywhere, and 'black-spit' was a common affliction:

The collier population is subject to a peculiar disease which is vulgarly called the black-spit, and by the faculty is dignified by the Greek term melanosis. It is a wasting of the lungs occasioned, as is supposed, by the inhaling of the coal-dust while working, and the expectoration is as black as the coal-dust itself. Many strong men are cut off by it before they reach the age of forty ... Almost all the men are affected by it sooner or later, so as to be rendered unfit for any active exertion for years before they drop prematurely into the grave, between the ages of forty and sixty or sixty-five.
(*New Statistical Account*, Newton, Edinburghshire, 1840)

The harsh work also reduced the miners' life expectancy, as the Commissioners found:

26. ... in the thin-seam mines, more especially, the limbs become crippled and the body distorted; and in general, the muscular powers give way, and the workpeople are incapable of following their occupation, at an earlier period of life than is common in other branches of industry.
27. ... and each generation of this class of the population is commonly extinct soon after fifty.
(Children's Employment Commission (Mines), *Parliamentary Papers*, 1842, vol. XV, pp. 258–9)

It is only horse-work, and ruins the women; it crushes their haunches, bends their ankles, and makes them old women at 40.
(Children's Employment Commission, *Report on the Collieries and Iron Works in the East of Scotland*, 1842, vol. ii, p. 458)

Miners' wages and living conditions

Miners were generally better paid than, for example, factory workers at this time, mainly because the dangerous and unpleasant nature of their work made it difficult to attract workers. Other attractions were offered to the miner, apart from comparatively high wages:

> The colliers could not leave their work, but an old collier who was past labour, was allowed two pecks of meal per week, and he had his free house and garden, and likewise his firing, continued to him, the same as when working. Each collier has a free house and garden, a quantity of meal, proportioned to the number of his family at the rate of 10½d [4½p] per peck, and their firing. Each family, upon an average, consumes rather more than 7 cwt [356 kg] of coal a week ... a good collier can clear from £25 to £35 per annum. To the women and children who carry up the coals on their backs, the colliers pay 4d. for carrying 30 cwt [1.5 tonnes].
> (*Old Statistical Account*, 1793, vol. 8, p. 615, Alloa)

In spite of their comparatively high wages, miners tended to be rough, uncivilised people, living in small villages close to the mine in which they worked. Other people regarded miners as a race apart, because of the frequency of drunkenness and the ill-treatment of children in mining communities:

> 17. ... the conduct of the adult colliers to the Children and Young Persons who assist them is harsh and cruel ...
> 24. ... in many cases, particularly in some parts of Yorkshire, in Derbyshire, in South Gloucester, and very generally in the East of Scotland, the food is poor in quality, and insufficient in quantity; the Children themselves say that they have not enough to eat; and the Sub-Commissioners describe them as covered with rags, and state that the common excuse they make for confining themselves to their homes on the Sundays, instead of taking recreation in the fresh air, or attending a place of worship, is that they have no clothes to go in; so that in these cases, notwithstanding the intense labour performed by these Children, they do not procure even sufficient food and raiment: in general, however, the Children who are in this unhappy case are the Children of idle and dissolute parents, who spend the hard-earned wages of their offspring at the public-house.
> (Children's Employment Commission (Mines), *Parliamentary Papers*, 1842, vol. XV, pp. 256–8)

1842 Mines Act

Until 1840, these dreadful working conditions and their effects were not generally known to most people in Britain. Then, Lord Ashley persuaded the government to set up a Commission to investigate working conditions for women and children in the mines. The Commissioners published their Report in 1842, and the vivid descriptions and illustrations of the hardships and dangers facing mine workers shocked all who read them.

Ashley introduced a Bill which eventually passed Parliament to become the Mines Act of 1842. By the terms of this Act, no women or girls were to be employed underground, nor were boys under 10 years. Inspectors were appointed to ensure that mine owners kept to the terms of the Act, and to prevent boys under 15 years from operating the winding equipment which had been the cause of many accidents. However, not until 1850 could these inspectors report on the safety of the mines and the machinery used in them.

QUESTIONS

1   Using the extracts and illustrations, describe the work of each of the following, including the dangers and hardships which faced them in their work:
   (a) A hewer,   (b) A drawer,   (c) A trapper,   (d) A bearer.
2   Why are the miners described as dropping 'prematurely into the grave', and being 'extinct soon after fifty.'?
3   Can you offer an explanation for the drunkenness of many miners and their brutality towards their children?
4   (a) Note the terms of the 1842 Mines Act.
   (b) What other improvements would you think a mines reformer like Ashley would hope to achieve in conditions in the mines?
   (c) What improvements in the mines took place without legislation by Parliament?

ASSIGNMENT

Imagine you were investigating working conditions in the mines for the Commission of 1840–42. Write a report to the Commissioners, quoting interviews you have had with mine-workers, and giving your impressions of visits to different mines. State your suggestions for improvements you would like to see made.

6 Poverty and Health

The New Poor Law

The Corn Law of 1815 was supposed to protect British farmers from foreign competition. But even after 1815, there were serious difficulties and set-backs in British agriculture. More and more farm labourers had to work for very low wages, or lost their jobs altogether. The situation was worst in the south and south-east of England, where great numbers of labourers were receiving poor relief under the 'Speenhamland system'. In some places magistrates actually reduced poor relief payments to avoid raising the rates to a level which was too high for the rate-payers to bear. As a result, there were widespread disturbances by labourers throughout the south of England in 1830–1, sometimes known as the 'last labourers' revolt'.

After the parliamentary Reform Act of 1832, the Whig government turned its attention to the problem of poverty. In 1832, it appointed a Royal Commission to study the existing methods of poor relief, and to make suggestions for improvements. The Commissioners included such well-known men as Edwin Chadwick and Nassau Senior. They were especially concerned about payments made to the able-bodied poor under the Speenhamland system, known as 'outdoor' relief. (See Chapter 1.) In their Report of 1834, the Commissioners expressed their concern:

Outdoor relief – the Speenhamland system

> It is true, that by the last Parliamentary return [that for the year ending the 25 March 1832] the total amount of the money expended for the relief of the poor, [was] higher than for any year since the year 1820 . . .

They had noticed:

> . . . the progressive deterioration of the labourers in the pauperised districts, and the increasing anxiety of the principal rate-payers, as their burden becomes more oppressive, to shift it in some way . . .
> (*Poor Law Report*, 1834 p. 54)

In fact, the Commissioners had made up their minds before they began their investigation. They thought the old method of poor relief was too expensive for rate-payers, and that it made many labourers think there was little reason to work if they would get payments from the parish for not working. Therefore the Commissioners wanted a less expensive system which would not be attractive to the poor.

> The first and most essential of all conditions . . . is that his [the pauper's] situation . . . shall not be made really or apparently so eligible as the situation of the independent labourer of the lowest class. Throughout the evidence it is shown, that in proportion as the condition of any pauper is elevated above the condition of independent labourers, the condition of the independent class is depressed . . . Such persons, therefore, are under the strongest inducements to quit the less eligible class of labourers and enter the more eligible class of paupers.
> (*Poor Law Report*, 1834 p. 228)

Indoor relief – workhouses

The Commissioners wanted to abolish the system of 'outdoor' relief and in its place, introduce a system of 'indoor' relief.

> . . . The chief specific measures which we recommended are:
> First, . . . all relief whatever to able-bodied persons or to their families otherwise than in well-regulated workhouses, . . . shall be declared unlawful, and shall cease . . .
> At least four classes are necessary: (1) The aged and really impotent; (2) The children; (3) The able-bodied females; (4) The able-bodied males. Of whom we trust that the two latter will be the least numerous classes . . . and the requisite superintendence may be better obtained in separate buildings than under a single roof.
> (*Poor Law Report*, 1834, pp. 262, 306–7)

The aim was to provide useful work for the able-bodied poor in workhouses, but to make these workhouses as unpleasant as possible, to encourage even those who did not wish to work to find a job. The Commissioners intended separate workhouses for different types of poor people, but in practice this did not usually happen.

The government acted quickly, and included the proposals of the Poor Law

Commissioners in the Poor Law Amendment Act of 1834. Poor relief on the lines of the Speenhamland system was to be ended, and workhouses were to be set up for the poor. However, some exceptions were allowed:

1. Where such person shall require relief on account of sudden and urgent necessity.
2. Where such person shall require relief on account of any sickness, accident, or bodily or mental infirmity . . .
3. Where such person being a widow, shall be in the first six months of widowhood.
(Poor Law Amendment Act, 1834)

The 1834 Act did not work out in detail a new system of poor relief. It simply set out the principle of 'indoor' relief in a workhouse, and created a method of applying this principle in practice. No longer would each parish be responsible for its own poor relief. Instead, parishes would be grouped into Poor Law 'Unions' which would organise workhouses in their Union areas.

XXXVII . . . where any Parishes shall be united . . . for the Relief of the Poor, a Board of Guardians of the Poor for such Union shall be constituted and chosen, and the Workhouse or Workhouses of such Union shall be administered, by such Board of Guardians; and the Guardians shall be elected by the Ratepayers.
(Poor Law Amendment Act, 1834)

The government realised that parishes might object to being grouped in 'unions', so the Poor Law Amendment Act stated that rates for paying for poor relief could continue to be collected by each individual parish. Even after 1851, parishes were still responsible for bearing the cost of looking after their own poor.

QUESTIONS

1 Why did the Poor Law Commissioners want to abolish methods of poor relief which existed before 1834?
2 Why did they feel that the 'workhouse system' would be cheaper than 'outdoor' poor relief?
3 In the 1834 Poor Law Amendment Act, how did the government alter the suggestions of the Poor Law Commissioners?
4 (a) What was a Poor Law 'union'?

(b) How would a person become a Poor Law Guardian, and what did the job involve?

Life in the workhouse

Workhouses were first set up gradually in the agricultural south of England. There were so many poor people, however, that it was impossible to stop the payment of 'outdoor' relief altogether.

Some workhouses were run efficiently, and as humanely as possible, but in general life in the workhouse was very harsh. It was the worst workhouses, and the unpleasantness of life in them, which received the most attention. For instance, the Commissioners said that families should be split up: if wives and husbands were kept apart, there would be fewer pauper children to look after.

Art.9. The paupers, so far as the workhouse admits thereof, shall be classed as follows, . . .
Class 1. Men infirm through age or any other cause.
Class 2. Able-bodied men, and youths above the age of 15 years.
Class 3. Boys above the age of 7 years, and under that of 15.
Class 4. Women infirm through age or any other cause.
Class 5. Able-bodied women, and girls above the age of 15.
Class 6. Girls above the age of 7 years, and under that of 15.
Class 7. Children under 7 years of age.
To each class shall be assigned that ward or separate building and yard which may be best fitted for the reception of such class, and each class of paupers shall remain therein, without communication with those of any other class.
(Workhouse rules drawn up by the Commissioners; *First Report of the Poor Law Commissioners*, 1835)

The Commissioners laid down very strict rules for workhouses:

WORKHOUSE (Rules of Conduct)
Any Pauper who shall neglect to observe such of the regulations herein contained as are applicable to and binding on him:
Or who shall make any noise when silence is ordered to be kept;
Or shall use obscene or profane language; . . .
Or shall refuse or neglect to work, after having been required to do so; . . .
Or shall play at cards or other games of chance; . . .
Shall be deemed DISORDERLY.

Any pauper who shall within seven days, repeat any one or commit more than one of the offences specified . . .

Or shall by word or deed insult or revile the master or matron, or any other officer of the workhouse, or any of the Guardians; . . .

Or shall be drunk; . . .

Or shall wilfully disturb the other inmates . . .

Shall be deemed REFRACTORY.

(Poor Law Commission, *Seventh Annual Report*, 1841)

An inmate of the workhouse found to be 'refractory' (disobedient) or 'disorderly', could be punished by solitary confinement, or by a reduction in his or her diet. As the diet sheet for Stow Union in Suffolk shows, food was in any case strictly rationed, and the diet was meagre:

STOW UNION.

DIETARY
FOR ABLE-BODIED MEN AND WOMEN.

		BREAKFAST		DINNER					SUPPER	
		Bread.	Gruel.	Meat pudding with Vegetables	Suet pudding with Vegetables	Bread.	Cheese.	Broth.	Bread.	Cheese.
		oz.	Pints.	oz.	oz.	oz.	oz.	Pints.	oz.	oz.
SUNDAY	Men	6 7	1½			7 8	1		6 7	1
	Women	5	1½			7	1		5	1
MONDAY	Men	6 7	1½	16					6 7	1
	Women	5	1½	10					5	1
TUESDAY	Men	6 7	1½			7 8	1	1/2	6 7	1
	Women	5	1½			7	1	1/2	5	1
WEDNESDAY,	Men	6 7	1½	16					6 7	1
	Women	5	1½	12					5	1
THURSDAY	Men	6 7	1½			7 8	1		6 7	1
	Women	5	1½			7	1		5	1
FRIDAY	Men	6 7	1½	16					6 7	1
	Women	5	1½	19					5	1
SATURDAY	Men	6 7	1½			7 8		1½	6 7	1
	Women	5	1½			7		1½	5	1

Old People, of Sixty Years of Age, and upwards, to be allowed 1 oz. of Tea, 5 oz. of Butter, and 7 oz. of Sugar per Week, in lieu of Gruel, for Breakfast.

There were many more rules which caused great distress. In some workhouses, meals had to be eaten in silence; inmates could only receive visitors in the presence of a workhouse official; and permission might be granted to leave the workhouse only if the inmate was going to church. Also, all types of paupers were usually kept in the same workhouse, although this was not intended at first by the Commissioners. So the old and young, diseased and healthy, sane and lunatic, law-abiding and criminal, could mix freely. The work provided was often useless, although the Commissioners had said it was not to be 'repellent'.

One of the greatest scandals arose over conditions in the Andover Union:

> *Evidence of Charles Lewis, labourer*
> [Mr. Wakely] What work were you employed about when you were in the workhouse? *I was employed breaking bones.*
> Were other men engaged in the same work? — *Yes.*
> Was that the only employment you had? — *That was the only employment I had at the time I was there.*
>
> During the time you were so employed, did you ever see any men gnaw anything or eat anything from these bones? — *I have seen them eat marrow out of the bones.*
>
> Did they state why they did it? — *I really believe they were hungry.*
> Did you see any of the men gnaw the meat from the bones? — *Yes.*
> Did they use to steal the bones and hide them away? — *Yes.*
> (*Report from the Select Committee on the Andover Union*, 1846, p. 104)

Opposition to the New Poor Law

From 1837, workhouses began to be set up in the Midlands and the north of England – areas which were much more industrial than the south. Though the workhouses had been hated by the poor in the south, it was in the north that most opposition to the New Poor Law arose. Factory workers and hand-loom weavers were used to being unemployed at regular intervals when trade was bad and fewer workers were needed. They depended on 'outdoor' poor relief payments to keep them going through these periods of unemployment. For the workers of the north, the New Poor Law meant long and regular periods in a workhouse instead of on 'outdoor' relief. To make matters worse, the new system was begun in the north just when trading difficulties were causing high unemployment. The workhouse system could not cope with the number of unemployed, as the Nottingham Guardians discovered:

. . . it soon became evident that a necessity would speedily arise for relieving more persons than could be provided for within the walls of the workhouses, and, . . . we felt it to be our duty to authorise . . . the Guardians that the rule which prohibited them from giving relief to able-bodied male persons except in the workhouse should be suspended whenever they should find the pressure [caused] a necessity for so doing. Preparation was thus made for placing the Guardians in a situation to meet the whole difficulty . . . of affording the necessary relief to such destitute persons as might be unable to maintain themselves when thrown out of work.
(Third Annual Report of the Poor Law Commissioners', 1837, *Parliamentary Papers*, 1837, xxxi)

There was tremendous opposition to the workhouses, or 'Bastilles' as they were nicknamed after the infamous Paris prison destroyed during the French Revolution. It came not only from the poor and unemployed, but also from such well-known men as the Todmorden factory owner John Fielden, the Radical Richard Oastler, and the Rev. J.R. Stephens, who put the case against workhouses in this way:

The people were not going to stand this, and he would say, that sooner than wife and husband, and father and son, should be sundered and dungeoned, and fed on 'skillee', – sooner than wife or daughter should wear the prison dress – sooner than that – Newcastle ought to be, and should be – one blaze of fire, with only one way to put it out, and that with the blood of all who supported this abominable measure . . .
(Extract from a speech by the Rev. J.R. Stephens on the New Poor Law, January 1838; in R.G. Gammage, *History of the Chartist Movement*, 1854, pp. 64–5)

Attacks on 'Bastilles' began to take place, such as the one at Stockport in 1842. Even John Fielden was willing to give up peaceful ways of opposing the workhouse system, and turn to violence. The Poor Law Commissioners presented the following evidence in their fifth Annual Report in 1839:

To oppose force to force we are not yet prepared; but if the people of this and the surrounding districts are to be driven to the alternative of either doing so, or surrendering their local government into the hands of an unconstitutional board of lawmakers, the time may not be far distant when the

experiment may be tried, and I would warn those who provoke the people to such a combat of the danger they are incurring.
(From a placard signed by John Fielden, reported in the *Fifth Annual Report of the Poor Law Commissioners*, 1839, p. 31–4)

The Commissioners themselves described one serious disturbance:

> In Todmorden Union, immediately on the introduction of the new system, an attempt was made by the partners of one manufactory . . . to prevent the peacable operation of the law, by throwing the whole of their work-people at once out of employment, and closing their works . . .
>
> On the 16th November last two constables from Halifax, who were employed in executing a warrant of distress upon the overseer of Langfield, were violently assaulted and overpowered by a concourse of persons, the first assembling of which was accompanied by the ringing of a bell in one of Messrs. Fielden's factories, from which a large number of work-people issued, and took part in the riot which ensued . . .
>
> Such was the state of excitement and alarm occasioned by these unfortunate proceedings that the magistrates . . . deemed it expedient on two occasions to call out a military force of the constables while engaged in making prisoners of some of the workmen in Messrs. Fielden's mills. It has also appeared essential to the security of the neighbourhood that a combined force of infantry and cavalry should be stationed at Todmorden for the present.
> (*Fifth Annual Report of the Poor Law Commissioners*, 1839, pp. 31–4)

In many areas of the north of England, the workhouse system could not be introduced. This was more because of the very large numbers of unemployed than the opposition to the New Poor Law. The payment of 'outdoor' relief continued, although it was often in return for hard labour such as stone breaking. Perhaps the harshness of living in a workhouse has been exaggerated, since not all workhouse overseers could have been cruel and brutal. Yet in his book in 1852, Robert Paisley found that Britain treated its poor much worse than other countries treated their own poor people:

> . . . The Workhouse as now organised is a reproach and disgrace peculiar to England; nothing corresponding to it is to be found throughout the whole of

the Continent of Europe. In France, the medical patients of our Workhouses would be found in 'hospitaux'; the infirm aged poor would be in 'hospices'; and the blind, the idiot, the lunatic, the bastard child and the vagrant would similarly be placed in an appropriate but separate establishment . . . It is at once equally shocking to every principle of reason and every feeling of humanity that all these varied forms of wretchedness should thus be crowded together into one common abode; . . .

(Robert Paisley *Pauperism and Poor Laws*, 1852)

Working class opposition to the New Poor Law was so great that, when those who opposed the Poor Law turned also to supporting the Chartist movement, Chartism was turned from an unimportant protest group into a mass movement. (See Chapter 7.)

QUESTIONS

1 Make a list of all the unpleasant features of life in a workhouse.
  (a) Why did the Commissioners want life in a workhouse to be unattractive?
  (b) What evidence is there of attempts to keep down the cost of the new system?
  (c) What evidence is there of useless work being given to the inmates?
2 Why was it possible to introduce the New Poor Law into the south of England, but not into the north?
3 What features of workhouse life did the Rev. J.R. Stephens oppose?
4. (a) How did John Fielden justify the use of force against the workhouse system?
    (b) How did he organise opposition to it?
    (c) Show that the magistrates regarded the situation as very serious.
5 What particular fault did Robert Paisley find with the New Poor Law?

ASSIGNMENTS

A. If you and your family had lived in the late 1830s or in the 1840s and had been admitted to a workhouse, describe how each of you would have been treated.
B. Imagine you were one of the Poor Law Commissioners making a report to the government in 1840 on the progress made in introducing the New Poor Law. What would you have said?
C. Summarise the arguments for and against (i) the Speenhamland system. (ii) the Poor Law of 1834.

Public Health

Living conditions in industrial towns

As we saw in Chapter 1, the Industrial Revolution led to the rapid growth of towns and cities in Britain in the first half of the nineteenth century. New houses, from cottages to tenements, were built as rapidly and cheaply as possible for factory workers. The builders had no concern for the people who were to be housed. The result was substandard housing lacking any water supply or sanitation, and built of such shoddy materials that it quickly decayed into slums.

Local authorities were taken by surprise at these sudden developments. Their towns were expanding so quickly that they could not provide proper drainage, sewerage and street cleansing for the new areas of housing. Also, local authorities usually had no powers to insist on proper standards of building, as John Robertson, a surgeon, reported in 1840:

> Manchester has no building Act, and hence, with the exception of certain central streets, over which the Police Act gives the Commissioners power, each proprietor builds as he pleases. New cottages . . . huddled together row behind row, may be seen springing up in many parts, . . . the authorities cannot interfere. A cottage row may be badly drained, the streets may be full of pits, brimful of stagnant water, the receptacle of dead cats and dogs, yet no-one may find fault.
> (John Robertson, *Report of the Committee on the Health of Towns*, xi, 1840)

The result was uncontrolled building and unplanned towns. Dr. J.P. Kay reported on the appalling living conditions which existed in Manchester in 1832:

> The greatest portion of those districts inhabited by the labouring population, . . . are of very recent origin; and from want of proper police [i.e. local authority] regulations are untraversed by common sewers. The houses are ill soughed [drained], often ill ventilated, unprovided with privies, and in consequence, the streets which are narrow, unpaved, and worn into deep ruts, become the common receptacle of mud, refuse, and disgusting ordure . . .
>
> This district . . . is surrounded on every side by some of the largest factories of the town, whose chimneys vomit forth dense clouds of smoke, which hang heavily over this insalubrious region.
> (J.P. Kay, *The Moral and Physical Condition of the Working Classes in Manchester*, 1832, pp. 12–34)

There were several particularly serious problems:

Sewage disposal

Since there were no proper sewers in most areas, human waste was disposed of in cesspools, dunghills or open sewers in the 'courts' between rows of houses, or else dumped directly into a river. In Glasgow, it was reported:

> There were no privies or drains there, and the dungheaps received all the filth which the swarm of wretched inhabitants could give; and we learnt that a considerable part of the rent of the houses was paid by the produce of dungheaps.
> (Dr. Neil Arnott's account of Glasgow slums, *Parliamentary Papers*, 1842, vol. 26, p. 24)

Cesspools were emptied and dunghills cleared at night because of the smells they raised, by men known as 'muck majors'.

Water supply

The houses of industrial workers had no running water, so water for drinking, cooking and washing was scarce. Water was usually obtained from a stand-pipe in the street, owned by a water company who sold the water at certain times of the day. But even when water was available, not every household owned the buckets or other containers suitable for storing it. In 1840, it was reported:

> ... There is a good supply of water for the poor, if they had the means of preserving it. The water is turned on a certain number of hours during the day ... the poor go to the tap for it; ... and each poor person fetches as much as they have pans to receive; but they are not well supplied with these articles, and in consequence they are frequently out of water. It is not sufficient for washing, or anything of that kind.
> (J. Riddall Wood, *Parliamentary Papers*, 1840, vol. XI, p. 132)

Often, water was taken from polluted rivers or other sources:

> ... there is a great deal of broken ground, in which there are pits; the water accumulates in those pits, and of course at the fall of the year there is a good deal of water in them, in which there have been thrown dead dogs and cats, and a great many offensive articles. The water is nevertheless used for culinary purposes. I could not believe this at first ...
> (Riddall Wood, *Parliamentary Papers*, 1840, vol. XI, p. 132)

Collecting water

The River Thames was used as a source of drinking water by Londoners, despite also being used as a sewer for the city!

It was not only the industrial towns of Britain which suffered such atrocious conditions, as the Provost of Inverness confirmed in 1842:

> Inverness is a nice town, situated in a most beautiful country . . . The people are, generally speaking, a nice people, but their sufferance of nastiness is past endurance. Contagious fever is seldom or ever absent; . . .
> . . . There are very few houses in the town which can boast of either water-closet or privy . . . Hence there is not a street, lane or approach to it that is not disgustingly defiled at all times, so much so as to render the whole place an absolute nuisance.
> (Dr. J.I. Nichol, Provost of Inverness, *Parliamentary Papers*, 1842, vol. 26, p. 43)

Lack of recreation

There were hardly any facilities for recreation so it was impossible for the inhabitants of the industrial areas to escape from their dreadful environment:

> Manchester has no public park or other grounds where the population can

walk and breathe the fresh air. New streets are rapidly extending in every direction, and those who live in more populous quarters can seldom hope to see the green face of nature.

(John Robertson, surgeon, in *Report of the Committee on the Health of Towns*, vol. xi, 1840)

Disease and death

Filthy living conditions and polluted water supplies cause disease, as we are now well aware. In the early nineteenth century, people were becoming aware of the connection between dirt and disease, but they did not know about the existence of germs, the actual cause of the disease. No wonder, then, that disease was always present to some extent in industrial towns. In some years, there were severe epidemics which claimed thousands of lives. In 1848–9, 15 000 people died in London alone.

In his book *The Condition of the Working Class in England*, Frederick Engels described the effects of epidemics throughout Britain:

It [fever] is to be found in the working people's quarters of all great towns and cities . . . though it naturally seeks out single victims in better districts also. In London it has now prevailed for a considerable time; its extraordinary violence in the year 1837 gave rise to the report already referred to . . . In the damp, dirty regions of the north, south, and east districts of London, this disease raged with extraordinary violence . . . This malignant fever is to be found in Manchester; in the worst quarters of the Old Town, Ancoats, Little Ireland, etc. it is rarely extinct . . . In Scotland and Ireland . . . it rages with a violence that surpasses all conception. . . . In Edinburgh about 6000 persons were attacked by the fever during the epidemic of 1817, and about 10 000 in that of 1837 . . .

But the fury of the epidemic in all former periods seems to have been child's play in comparison with its ravages after the crisis of 1842. One sixth of the whole . . . population of Scotland was seized by the fever, and the infection was carried . . . with fearful rapidity from one locality to another. . . . In Glasgow, twelve per cent of the population were seized in the year 1843; 32 000 persons, of whom thirty-two per cent perished . . . The illness reached a crisis on the seventh and fifteenth days; on the latter, the patient usually became yellow . . .

(F. Engels, *The Condition of the Working Class in England*)

A COURT FOR
KING CHOLERA.

The 'fever' which Engels described was typhus. It was carried from person to person by lice. Cholera was another killer disease. It was caused by germs in infected water, cesspools and dungheaps. The worst cholera epidemics in this period were in 1831–2 and 1848–9. Other major diseases of the time were consumption and scarlet fever.

Burials

Cemeteries and burial grounds quickly became overcrowded because the population was growing so rapidly and the death rate was so high. Delays of days and even weeks in carrying out burials added to the danger of disease. Families had to keep bodies in their homes during that period, often because they had to save up to pay for the burial. Yet Engels was surprised that the situation was no worse:

> When one remembers under what conditions the working-people live, when one thinks how crowded their dwellings are, how every nook and corner swarms with human beings, how sick and well sleep in the same room, in the same bed, the only wonder is that a contagious disease like this fever does not spread yet farther. And when one reflects how little medical assistance the sick have at command, . . . and ignorant of the most ordinary precautionary measures, the mortality seems actually small.
> (Engels, *The Condition of the Working Class in England*)

QUESTIONS

1 (a) Why was there such a great demand for more housing at the start of the nineteenth century?
(b) How was it possible for housing to be built of such poor quality, lacking sanitation and running water?
2 List the different sources of disease which faced the people living in the growing towns and cities.
3 (a) Why were working people in more danger than other classes?
(b) Why did disease spread so rapidly?
(c) Give three reasons why Engels was surprised there was not more disease.

The Work of Edwin Chadwick

As we have seen (page 84), Edwin Chadwick was among those responsible for the New Poor Law of 1834 and a Poor Law Commissioner. In his work as a Poor Law Commissioner he became aware of the worsening living conditions in the towns, and led the campaign to improve public health and wipe out disease. To find out exactly what living conditions were like for working people, he appointed Doctors Kay, Arnott and Southwood-Smith to investigate housing conditions in East London. The registration of births, marriages and deaths had become compulsory in 1836, and these records helped their work greatly. The evidence produced by these men revealed for the first time to the middle class and the government the conditions in which most working people lived.

As a result, the government set up a Royal Commission in 1839, again headed by Chadwick, to carry out a nation-wide survey. Chadwick's 'Report on the Sanitary Conditions of the Labouring Population of Great Britain' in 1842 was the most detailed examination of the problem up to that time.

Chadwick's findings

First, as to the extent and operation of the evils which are the subject of this enquiry –

That the various forms of epidemic, endemic and other diseases caused, or aggravated or propagated chiefly amongst the labouring classes by atmospheric impurities produced by decomposing animal and vegetable substances, by damp and filth, and close overcrowded dwellings prevail amongst the population in every part of the kingdom.

...that where those circumstances are removed by drainage, proper cleansing, better ventilation, and other means of diminishing atmospheric impurity, the frequency and intensity of such disease is abated; and where the removal of the noxious agencies appears to be complete, such disease almost entirely disappears...

That the formation of all habits of cleanliness is obstructed by defective supplies of water.

(*Parliamentary Papers*, 1842, vol. 26, pp. 369–372)

Chadwick then showed the effect such conditions had on the health of people in towns, and compared the health of town dwellers with those in the country:

You have seen the returns of the average ages of death amongst the different classes of people in Manchester and Rutland:

Average age of death	In Manchester	In Rutland (shire)
Professional persons and gentry and families	38	52
Trademen and their families	20	41
Mechanics, labourers and families	17	38

(Evidence presented in Chadwick's 'Report on the Sanitary Conditions of the Labouring Population of Great Britain', 1842)

Chadwick's recommendations

...As to the means by which the present sanitary condition of the labouring classes may be improved:

The primary and most important measures, and at the same time the most practicable, and within the recognised province of public administration, are drainage, the removal of all refuse of habitations, streets, and roads, and the improvement of the supplies of water...

> That for the prevention of the disease occasioned by defective ventilations, and other causes of impurity in places of work and other places where large numbers are assembled, and for the general promotion of the means necessary to prevent disease, that it would be good economy to appoint a district medical officer independent of private practice, and with the securities of special qualifications and responsibility to initiate sanitary measures . . .
>
> ('Report from Poor Law Commissioners on an Enquiry into the Sanitary Condition of the Labouring Population of Great Britain', *Parliamentary Papers*, 1842, pp 369–72)

Chadwick emphasised that bad living conditions did not exist only in industrial towns, and that high death rates did not apply only to the working classes. He pointed out that a national body would need to be set up to organise sanitary improvements, because huge engineering schemes would be required to improve drainage and sewerage throughout the country.

Although genuinely concerned with the health of the people, Chadwick also stressed the need for economy, as he had done with the New Poor Law:

> That the expense of public drainage, of supplies of water laid on in houses, and of means of improving cleansing would be a pecuniary gain, by diminishing the existing charges attendant on sickness and premature mortality.
>
> ('Sanitary Condition of the Labouring Population of Great Britain', *Parliamentary Papers*, 1842, vol. 26, pp. 369–72)

He said that if the government followed his suggestions, the effect would be dramatic:

> That by the combinations of all these arrangements, it is probable that, . . . an increase of 13 years at least, may be extended to the whole [life] of the labouring classes . . .
>
> ('Sanitary Condition of the Labouring Population', *Parliamentary Papers*, 1842)

The 1848 Public Health Act and the Board of Health

The government did little in the next few years to improve public health, except to appoint another Royal Commission in 1843, in spite of all Chadwick's shocking evidence about sanitary conditions in Britain. This meant that local authorities were left to find their own solutions to problems which were afflicting all large towns and cities. Some improvements were made: for example, Manchester had a reasonable water supply by 1847; Liverpool appointed a Medical Officer of Health in 1847; and London followed in 1848. But these were limited, local measures, and living conditions in most towns remained dreadful.

In 1848, Parliament at last passed a Public Health Act, but only because there was a particularly severe outbreak of cholera in that year. This was an important breakthrough in public health, even though it was not to last very long. The Act set up a permanent Central Board of Health in London. (Chadwick and Lord Ashley were two of its original members.) Also, local Boards of Health could be set up in areas where either 10 per cent of the rate-payers asked for them, or where the death rate was greater than 23 per 1000 per year. (In Britain, the death rate varied from 15 per 1000 to 30 per 1000, with the very worst areas reaching 60 per 1000.) This Public Health Act gave local Boards the right to appoint an Officer of Health, and to levy rates for the following purposes:

> XLVI. . . . the Local Boards of Health shall cause the sewers vested in them by this Act to be covered so as not to be a nuisance or injurious to health, and to be properly cleared, cleansed and emptied . . .
>
> XLIX. . . . it shall not be lawful to erect any house . . . unless and until a covered drain . . . be constructed.
>
> LXXX. . . . the local board of health may provide their districts with such a supply of water as may be proper for the purposes of this Act and for private use to the residents.
>
> (Public Health Act, 1848)

The local Boards of Health had the power to carry out sanitary improvements and to follow suggestions by the Central Board in London if they wished. But they were not compelled to do so by the Act. This meant that areas with active local Boards, such as Darlington, saw great sanitary improvements. Dr. S.E. Piper, the Medical Officer of Health for Darlington, was able to report that if diseases broke out:

> Their coming was looked for, and all the appliances that science could devise were put into requisition to meet the calamity. Water had been intro-duced into our streets . . . new sewers and drains . . . were in effective opera-tion . . . cesspools abolished . . . and an efficient force of scavengers em-ployed in removing all refuse from our streets . . . when epidemic diseases again appeared they could not maintain a footing in the old haunts where

they formerly lingered . . . As an example of the change that has been effected . . . I may mention that the death-rate has fallen from 68 to 23 per 1000.

(Annual Report (1855) of Dr. Stephen Edward Piper, Medical Officer of Health for Darlington, 1851–82)

However, many local Boards were less active, and merely made temporary appointments when an emergency arose:

That in consequence of the Cholera having for some days ceased in this District, the Board consider they may dispense with the services of Dr. Camps.

(Minutes of the Bridgend, Glamorgan, Board of Health, 20 November, 1854)

At the Central Board of Health, Chadwick worked hard to introduce the new methods he felt to be right. One of the improvements he introduced was the use of narrow pipe sewers, along which sewage could more easily be flushed, in place of the large, brick-lined sewers which had existed until then.

Opposition to the Public Health Act

There was a considerable amount of opposition to the Board of Health. Many local authorities resented what they saw as interference in local affairs by the government. Other local interests, such as the water companies, objected to the Boards of Health taking over their work. The Central Board was very well aware of such opposition when it reported in 1854:

> ... We are aware that, in the discharge of [our] duties ... we have unavoidably interfered with powerful interests, which have the immediate means of making themselves heard by members of Government and by Parliament.
>
> ... we have been under the necessity of stating facts with relation to the inefficiency of former works, and their effect in aggravating existing evil.
>
> ... The scheme we proposed for extra-mural burial endangered ... cemetery companies and the entire body of trading undertakers.
>
> ... The report in condemnation of the present ... supply of water to the Metropolis, necessarily excited the hostility of the existing water companies.
>
> ... Accounts of particular stoppages of pipe sewers were promulgated without any reference to the circumstances which showed that they might have been expected to stop; without any notice of the large proportion of good work executed ...
>
> ('Report of the Board of Health on its work', *Parliamentary Papers*, 184/ xxxv, pp. 48–54)

The Central Board was often unfairly blamed for actually *causing* disease to spread:

> ... While the new works were in progress and approaching completion, an extraordinary epidemic which has prevailed in different parts of the country, in places where there are no new works whatsoever, attacked the higher class of houses in Croydon, those with old as well as those with new works. The disease was immediately ascribed to the operation of the new drainage works, although the first and most severe visitation of the epidemic was at the distance of upwards of three-quarters of a mile from the places where the works were going on.
>
> (Report of the Board of Health on its work', *Parliamentary Papers*, 184/ xxxv, pp. 48–54)

By 1854, the Board was able to report that considerable progress had been made.

We have now to state that 284 towns have memorialised and petitioned in form for the application of the Act. Of these, . . . the requisite forms and proceedings prescribed by the Act, have been complied with in 182 . . . comprising altogether a total population . . . of upwards of two millions – (2 100 000)
('Report of the Board of Health on its work', *Parliamentary Papers*, 184/ xxv, p. 13)

Opposition to the Board of Health proved too strong, however. Its enemies used their influence in Parliament and with the government to force Chadwick's resignation in 1853, and to cause the Board of Health's affairs to be wound up in 1854.

QUESTIONS

1 (a) Where did Chadwick show that life expectancy was the lowest?
(b) Who had the lowest life expectancy, according to Chadwick?
(c) What reasons did Chadwick give for the low life expectancy in towns?
(d) How did he show that such early deaths were not inevitable?
2 What measures did Chadwick advise the government to take?
3 Why did he maintain his suggestions would actually save *money?*
4 (a) What powers were given to local Boards of Health by the Public Health Act of 1848?
(b) Why did the creation of a Central Board of Health, and local Boards of Health, not lead to immediate improvements in public health all over Britain?
5 Why was there opposition to the Public Health Act of 1848 by certain
(a) local authorities; (b) rate-payers; (c) owners of property?

ASSIGNMENTS

A. Imagine you had been assigned to investigate living conditions in a particular town for Chadwick's 'Report on the Sanitary Conditions of the Labouring Population' in 1842. Write a letter to Chadwick outlining the conditions you have discovered, and making your suggestions for necessary improvements.
B. Summarise the arguments which existed in the 1840s for *and* against *a Public Health Act.*
C. The Board of Health ceased to exist in 1854, and there were no more far-reaching public health measures until the 1870s. Were the years from 1838–54 therefore wasted ones for those who wished to improve public health?

7 Working Class Movements

The Industrial Revolution brought about many changes. The domestic system of manufacturing goods was replaced by the factory system; people flocked to work in the factories leading to the growth of industrial towns (see Chapter I). Factory workers found many reasons to complain about their new lives. In the old days they had been able to work at their own pace in their cottages; now they were herded together in factories and forced to work long hours for little pay, in grim conditions (see Chapter 5). At night they struggled home to the crowded slums, huddled round the factories (see Chapter 6).

Some workers thought that the factory owners would always illtreat their workers and pay them as little as possible, so that they could make as much profit as possible. There seemed to be only two ways of putting an end to such treatment. First of all, workers could join together or *combine* to force their employer to give them better conditions; or they could try to get working people into Parliament so that laws could be passed to help them. The first part of this chapter deals with the attempts by workers to form combinations, or, as they are more usually called, *trade unions*; later on, the chapter deals with attempts to get workers elected to Parliament – the movement referred to as *Chartism*.

TRADE UNIONS

Combination Acts, 1799–1825

The number of trade unions grew quickly in the years before 1800. Trade unions were not a new idea, but the Industrial Revolution encouraged them to spread since many people now worked and lived together, and shared the same problems. Factory owners and the government viewed these early trade unions with suspicion, and did their best to halt their growth. After the French revolution in 1789 the government was particularly worried about any combination of discontented people, and it was this fear that led to the Combination Acts of 1799–1800:

> BE IT THEREFORE ENACTED that from and after the passing of this Act all contracts, covenants and agreements whatsoever, in writing, . . . by or between any . . . workmen within this kingdom for obtaining an advance of wages of them . . . or for lessening or altering . . . their usual hours of time or working, or for decreasing the quantity of work, or for preventing or hindering any person or persons from employing whomsoever he, she or they shall think proper to employ . . . shall be declared to be illegal, null and void . . .
> (Combination Act, 1800, 40 Geo. III c. 100)

Despite the Combination Laws, trade unions continued to exist in secret. This was not a satisfactory state of affairs, as Francis Place pointed out:

> The laws against combinations . . . induced workers to break and disregard the laws. They made them hate their employers with a rancour which nothing else could have produced. And they made them hate those of their own class who refused to join them, to such an extent as . . . to seek to do them mischief.
> (G. Wallas, *Life of Francis Place 1771–1854*, 1898)

Place and the Radical M.P., Joseph Hume, succeeded in persuading the government to set up a committee to look at the working of the Combination Laws. Place made sure that he saw the witnesses first:

> The delegates from the working people had reference to me, and I opened my house to them . . . I examined and cross-examined them; took down the leading particulars of each case and then arranged the matter as briefs for Mr Hume; and as a rule, for the guidance of the witnesses, a copy was given to each . . . The workmen were not easily managed. I had to discuss everything with them most carefully, to arrange and prepare everything, and so completely did these things occupy my time, that for more than three months I had hardly time for rest.
> (Wallas, *Life of Francis Place*, pp. 211–216)

The result of all this careful preparation was that a bill repealing the Combination Laws passed through Parliament almost unnoticed in 1824. In that year an upsurge in industry and trade reached a great peak, as the demand for British factory goods increased. A flood of strikes followed and the government acted quickly. They decided that the 1824 Act repealing the Combination Laws had gone too far, so they passed an Amending Act in 1825. This Act limited the freedoms newly gained by workers, but left them with certain important rights:

> ... this Act shall not extend to subject any persons to punishment, who shall meet together for the sole purpose of consulting upon and determining the rate of Wages or prices, or the hours or time which he or they shall work in any manufacture, trade or business ...
> (Combination Act, 1825–6 Geo. IV, c. 129)

QUESTIONS

1 (a) *What actions were made illegal by the Combination Laws of 1799–1800?*
   (b) *What would be the overall effect of the laws on trade unions?*
2 (a) *Give three reasons why Francis Place disliked the Combination Laws.*
   (b) *Describe carefully Place's part in bringing about repeal of the laws.*
3 (a) *What did the members of the government assume to be the reason for the great number of strikes in 1824–25?*
   (b) *Can you suggest any other reason to explain the strikes at that time?*
4 *What "important rights" did the Amending Act of 1825 leave to trade unionists?*

ASSIGNMENT

Imagine you were a factory worker in the early nineteenth century. Write a letter to a friend explaining why you had been opposed to the Combination Laws of 1799–1800, and what you did to get round them. Describe your reaction to the Repeal Act of 1824, and give your opinion of the 1825 Act.

Attempts to form a general union

The number of trade unions increased after the Acts of 1824–25, and some people now supported a new idea. They wanted *all* workers to join together in one giant trade union, which would be strong enough to force the employers and government to give in to their demands. Robert Owen, the factory reformer, was a supporter of this idea of a general trade union.

> Strikes after strikes in thick succession rise. The evil of all these engagements is, that they are partial; they are merely skirmishes, which may for a

season annoy the enemy, but can never accomplish anything conclusive, for
the benefit of industry at large . . . By a general union they [the working
classes] might provide themselves with every species of power; and by a
general strike they might bring their superiors to any terms of accommodation.
(Robert Owen in *The Crisis*, 3 May 1834)

Owen hoped that the general union would open the way to a new world in which
there would no longer be rich and poor, or bosses and workers. Instead everybody
would work together and help each other, and the horrors of the factory system
would be forgotten. Owen became one of the leading influences in the best known
attempt at a general union, the Grand National Consolidated Trade Union
(GNCTU) which was formed in 1834. It grew very rapidly, and soon claimed a
membership of over half a million. Within months, however, it had collapsed.

Failure of the GNCTU

It is now clear that although the GNCTU claimed such a large membership, few
people or groups actually paid any subscription fees. The membership was
divided, since many workers disliked the idea of paying fees, or going on strike
for the benefit of workers in another trade. In addition, the GNCTU faced strong
opposition from employers, many of whom made their workers sign the 'Document' as a condition of employment:

The Document

We, the undersigned . . . do hereby declare that we are not in any way con-
nected with the General Union . . . and that we do not and will not contribute
to the support of such members of the said [union] as are or may be out of
work as a consequence of belonging to such union.
(*Brief History of the Operative Building Trades Union*, 1835)

The Tolpuddle Martyrs

The GNCTU was firmly opposed by the government. Its attitude is seen in the
famous case of the 'Tolpuddle Martyrs' – six farm labourers from Dorset who
formed a branch of the union. The local magistrates heard about it through a spy
and, encouraged by the government, brought the men to trial. George Loveless,
one of the six, explained how the local employers had agreed that their wages
should be the same as those in other areas – ten shillings (50p) – but gradually,
that wage had been reduced:

Later we were reduced to seven shillings [35p] per week, and shortly after our employers told us they must lower us to six shillings [30p] per week. The labouring men consulted together what had better be done, as they knew it was impossible to live honestly on such scanty means. I had seen at different times accounts of Trade Societies; I told them of this and they willingly consented to form a friendly society among the labourers. I enquired of a brother how to proceed, and shortly after two delegates from a Trade Society paid us a visit, formed a Friendly Society among the labourers, and gave us directions how to proceed. This was about the latter end of 1833.

Nothing particular happened from this time to the 21st of February, 1834, when placards were posted up at the most conspicuous places, threatening to punish with seven years transportation any man who should join the Union. This was the first time that I had heard of any law being in existence to forbid such societies . . .

As to the trial, I need not mention but little; the grand jury appeared to ransack heaven and earth to get some clue against us, but in vain; our masters were enquired of to know if we were not idle, or attended public houses or some other fault in us; and much as they were opposed to us, they had common honesty to declare that we were good labouring servants, and that they never heard of any complaint against us, and when nothing whatever could be raked together, the unjust and cruel judge, Williams, ordered us to be tried for mutiny and conspiracy, under an Act of 1797, for the suppression of mutiny among the marines and seamen . . . at the Nore [a naval base].

(George Loveless, *Victims of Whiggery*, 1837)

The six were sentenced to seven years transportation, and, despite the great outcry and protest which followed, were not given free pardons until 1838.

QUESTIONS

1 (a) Why did some workers want to form a general trade union?
(b) What did Robert Owen believe would be the immediate result of a general strike?
(c) What sort of 'new world' did Owen then hope to create?
2 (a) What was the 'Document'?
(b) What effect do you think the sentence of the 'Tolpuddle Martyrs' would have on other workers who had considered joining the union?
(c) Briefly list four reasons why the GNCTU collapsed.

A meeting of protest against the deportation of the Tolpuddle Martyrs.

ASSIGNMENT

Write a newspaper report on the trial of the 'Tolpuddle Martyrs'. Give your report a suitable headline, and then divide it into sections – why the government was against the GNCTU; the reason the farm workers formed their society; the sort of men they were; the fairness of the trial; the sentence; the reaction of other working men.

Chartism

By the mid-1830s, life and work for most working people was as unpleasant as ever. Many of them had hoped that the Whigs would pass reforms to make things better, but this had not happened. Working people were disappointed by the 1832 Reform Act (see Chapter 4), the 1833 Factory Act (see Chapter 5), and most of all by the hated Poor Law Amendment Act of 1834 (see Chapter 6). The high hopes which they had pinned on trade unions like the GNCTU also collapsed with the disasters of 1834.

> It was the fond expectation of the friends of the people that a remedy for the greater part, if not for the whole, of their grievances would be found in the Reform Act of 1832. They have been bitterly and basely deceived ... The Reform Act has effected [brought about] the transfer of

power from one domineering faction [controlling group] to another, and left
the people helpless as before . . .
(The Chartist Petition, 1838; in R.G. Gammage, *History of the Chartist
Movement*, 1854, pp. 87–90)

Some people believed that the only way to improve matters was to get working
people elected to Parliament, which would then have to pass the laws the workers
wanted. Groups such as the London Working Men's Association, the Birmingham
Political Union and the factory workers of northern England and Scotland, supported this idea. In 1836, William Lovett of the London Working Men's Association summed up their demands in a document which became known as the People's Charter. The Charter contained six points which Lovett and his friends
wanted Parliament to pass as new laws. The movement which developed to persuade Parliament to accept the Six Points of the People's Charter became known
as *Chartism*, and its supporters, *Chartists*.

THE SIX POINTS
OF THE PEOPLE'S CHARTER

1. A vote for every man twenty-one years of age, of sound mind, and not
   undergoing punishment for crime.

2. The Ballot – To protect the elector in the exercise of his vote.

3. No Property Qualification for Members of Parliament – thus enabling the
   constituencies to return the man of their choice, be he rich or poor.

4. Payment of Members, thus enabling an honest tradesman, working man,
   or other person, to serve a constituency, when taken from his business to
   attend to the interests of the country.

5. Equal Constituencies, securing the same amount of representation for the
   same number of electors, instead of allowing small constituencies to
   swamp the votes of large ones.

6. Annual Parliaments, thus presenting the most effectual check to bribery
   and intimidation, since though a constituency might be bought once in
   seven years (even with the ballot), no purse could buy a constituency
   (under a system of universal suffrage) in each ensuing twelvemonth; and
   since members, when elected for a year only, would not be able to defy
   and betray their constituents as now.

Joseph Rayner Stephens, an outspoken Chartist leader, summed up the overall aim of the Six Points:

> This question of universal suffrage [vote for all men] is a knife and fork question, a bread and cheese question . . . if any man asks me what I mean by universal suffrage, I would answer that every working man in the land has the right to have a good coat on his back, a comfortable abode in which to shelter himself and his family, a good dinner upon his table, and no more work than is necessary for keeping him in good health and as much wages for that work as would keep him in plenty . . .
> (*Manchester and Salford Advertiser*, 25 March 1838)

QUESTIONS

1 *(a) Why were workers disappointed by the 1832 Reform Act?*
(b) Working people had hoped that the Reform Act would have provided a remedy for their grievances. How could it have done this?
(c) 'The Reform Act has effected the transfer of power from one domineering faction to another . . .' (i) Who are the two factions referred to here? (ii) How had this 'transfer of power' come about?
2 *(a) Why were working people disappointed by the Factory Act?*
(b) Why was the Poor Law Amendment Act 'hated'?
(c) What were the 'disasters' suffered by trades unions in 1834?
3 *Write down the Six Points of the Charter. Beside each, explain why the Chartists wanted that particular point made law.*

The first Chartist petition

The Chartists held public meetings throughout 1838. It was a hard year for many people, with rising unemployment, and people flocked to hear the Chartists. Feargus O'Connor, a fiery Irishman and owner of the northern England Radical newspaper, *Northern Star*, became their best-known speaker. *The Northern Star* spread Chartist ideas to a wide audience, and gave great publicity to their meetings.

It was decided that the best plan was to gather a great petition which would be presented to Parliament along with the People's Charter. While this was going on, a Chartist Convention was to meet in London. The Convention started its business in February 1839, with its members referring to themselves as M.C. – Member of Convention. Although the petition was not yet complete, it was already fairly clear that Parliament would reject it. Most of the discussion therefore centred on one vital point – what could the Chartists do next? There were two main proposals. First of all, Feargus O'Connor asked:

> Shall it be said, fellow countrymen, that four millions of men, capable of bearing arms, and defending their country against every foreign assailant, allowed a few domestic oppressors to enslave and degrade them?... We have resolved to obtain our rights 'peaceably if we may, forcibly if we must;' but woe to those who begin the warfare with the millions, or who forcibly resist their peaceful agitation for justice ...
> (*Northern Star*, 3 July 1847)

and William Lovett replied:

> The whole physical force agitation is harmful and injurious to the movement. Muskets are not what are wanted, but education and schooling of the working people. Stephens and O'Connor are shattering the movement ... O'Connor wants to take everything by storm, and to pass the Charter into law within a year. All this hurry and haste, this bluster and menace of armed opposition can only lead to ... the destruction of Chartism.
> (William Lovett, *Life and Struggles of William Lovett*, 1876)

In the end neither O'Connor's demand for *physical* force nor Lovett's insistence on *moral* force won the argument outright. Instead it was decided to hold a general strike lasting a month – the 'Sacred Month' – which, it was hoped, would finally persuade the government to make the People's Charter law. Feargus O'Connor realised the disadvantages of such a scheme:

> If I thought you could test the value of labour by a month's holiday, I would say have it ... But you know – you all know – that the baker will not bake, the butcher will not kill, and the brewer will not brew; and then what becomes of the millions of starving human beings?... Make your necessary arrangements; have a three days' holiday instead of a month's strike and what you fail to effect by it, would have been equally lost by the month ... but I never will, with a certainty of my own dinner, recommend a project which may cause millions to starve ...
> (*Northern Star*, 3 August 1839)

The petition was presented to Parliament in the summer of 1839, and, as expected, it was promptly rejected. The 'Sacred Month' received scarcely any support and fizzled out after a few days. A few outbreaks of violence occurred, the most serious at Newport in Wales. It was planned that several groups of Chartists would march on the town and capture it, but the authorities had troops ready, and in the battle which followed, as many as twenty people may have been killed. John Frost and the other leaders were sentenced to death, later reduced to transportation for life. Indeed, by 1840 most Chartist leaders, including Lovett and O'Connor, were in prison, and the movement, for the time being, disappeared from the head-lines.

QUESTIONS

1 (a) *Who was O'Connor referring to as "a few domestic oppressors"?*
   (b) *What do you think he hoped to achieve by his call for physical force?*
2 (a) *Why was Lovett opposed to physical force?*
   (b) *What did he propose instead?*
3 (a) *What were O'Connor's objections to the 'Sacred Month'?*
   (b) *Can you suggest any other reason why a strike at that particular time may not have been a good idea?*

The second petition and the 'Plug Plot'

In 1842, unemployment rose again and more factory workers in the north of England were thrown out of work. Support for Chartism revived and another petition was presented to Parliament, with three and a quarter million signatures – but once again it was rejected. Many people believed that this was the spark which set off a great wave of strikes:

> 'The Plug Plot' of 1842, as it is still called in Lancashire, began in reduction of wages by the manufacturers. The people advanced at last, to a wild general strike, and drew the plugs from the steam boilers so as to stop the work at the mills, and thus render labour impossible. The first meeting where the resolution was passed 'that all labour should cease until the People's Charter became the law of the land' was held on the 7th of August . . . In the course of a week, the resolution had been passed in nearly all the great towns of Lancashire, and tens of thousands had held up their hands in favour of it.
> (Thomas Cooper, *Life of Thomas Cooper by Himself*, 1879)

By the end of August, 1842, hunger had forced many strikers back to work, and the strike had collapsed. Employment prospects improved, especially with the demand for labourers on the new railways (see Chapter 9) and Chartism again went into decline.

QUESTIONS

1   Why did support for Chartism revive in 1842?
2   (a) What was the 'Plug Plot'?
*(b) The word 'plot' suggests these strikes were part of a prepared plan. Is
there any evidence above that this was so? Do you believe there really was a
plot?*
3   Why did support for Chartism decline again?

The Chartist Land Company

When the Chartists' political aims were defeated once again, O'Connor turned to
one of his other ideas which was intended to improve people's lives. He set up the
Chartist Land Company which was to buy land to create new communities. Workers could get a plot of land by buying shares in the company. They would escape
from the horrors of the factories and would live peaceful and contented lives
growing food and providing the necessities of life for each other. O'Connor did
his best to persuade people to join:

> Every acre was to yield on average such crops as no acre ever did yield
> except under the rarest combinations of favouring climate, consummate skill
> and unlimited manure – and then only occasionally. Every cow was to live
> for ever, was to give more milk than any save the most exceptional cow ever
> gave before, and was never to be dry. Every pig was to be a prime one,
> every goose to be a swan.
> (*Edinburgh Review*)

Five such communities were eventually set up, and one near London was called
O'Connorville after its founder. Unfortunately, it soon became obvious that
O'Connor knew little about agriculture and even less about how to run a company.
A government enquiry was ordered into the financial affairs of the company. It
discovered that O'Connor had mismanaged the entire scheme, although he had not
acted with criminal intent. Most of the settlers were forced to give up their plots,
and the company was wound up in 1852.

QUESTIONS

1   (a) What was the purpose of the Chartist Land Company?
(b) Why do you think it proved so popular at first?
2   Give two reasons why the plan failed.

The Chartist meeting on Kennington Common.

The third petition

Hard times returned in 1847. Many businesses collapsed and unemployment rose again, and Chartism received further encouragement from a revolution in France.

> Heroic citizens [of Paris]. The thunder notes of your victory have sounded across the Channel awakening the sympathies and hopes of every lover of liberty . . . The fire that consumed the throne of the royal traitor and tyrant will kindle the torch of liberty in every country in Europe.
> (*Northern Star*, 12 March 1848)

The overthrow of the King of France was followed by revolutions in nearly every other country in Europe. Encouraged by their success, the Chartists decided to make what they thought would be the last big effort. Another great petition was to be collected, and, after a mass meeting on Kennington Common in London, the Chartists would march on Parliament with their petition and demand that the Charter be made law.

The government was worried by this plan. It seemed that the revolutions on the Continent were going to spread to Britain. The Duke of Wellington was put in charge of the defences of the capital, and elaborate preparations were made:

> *April 6th* – All London is making preparations to encounter a Chartist row tomorrow. All the clerks in the different offices are ordered to be sworn in special constables and to constitute themselves into garrisons . . . and I am to

send down all my guns; in short we are to take a war-like attitude . . . Every gentleman in London is become a constable, and there is an organization of some sort in every district.

(In Strachey, L & Fulford, R (ed): *The Greville Memoirs*, 1936)

The preparations proved unnecessary. O'Connor had hoped for a crowd of 500 000, but in the end about 20 000 turned up. O'Connor was very frightened that violence would break out, and agreed with the police that he alone should take the petition to Parliament.

April 13th – Monday passed off with surprising quiet, and it was considered a most satisfactory demonstration on the part of the government, and the peaceable and loyal part of the community.

In the morning (a very fine day) everybody was on the alert; the parks were closed; our office was fortified . . . and all our guns were taken down to be used in the defence of the building. However about twelve o'clock crowds came streaming along Whitehall, going northward, and it was announced that all was over. The intended tragedy was rapidly changing into a ludicrous farce . . .

(*Greville Memoirs*)

The last great Chartist petition arrived quietly and without ceremony, delivered to Parliament in three cabs. This time Parliament took the trouble to study it:

The Hon. Member for Nottingham [Mr F. O'Connor] stated on presenting the petition, that 5 706 000 names were attached to it; but upon the most careful examination . . . the number of signatures has been ascertained to be 1 975 496. It is further evident to your Committee that on numerous consecutive sheets the signatures are in one and the same hand-writing. Your Committee also observed the names of distinguished individuals attached to the petition, who can scarcely be supposed to concur to its prayer; among which occurs the name of Her Majesty, as Victoria Rex, April 1st, F.M. Duke of Wellington, Sir Robert Peel, etc.

Your Committee have also observed . . . the insertion of numbers of names which are obviously fictitious, such as ''No Cheese'', ''Pug Nose'', ''Flat Nose''. There are others included, which your Committee do not hazard offending the House and the dignity and the decency of their own proceedings by reporting.

(Select Committee on Public Petitions, *Hansard*, 1849)

The third petition was rejected and became a public joke. Trade improved, the workers turned again to the trade unions, and the Chartist movement faded out of existence.

It had not been a complete waste of time, however. Later in the nineteenth and early twentieth century, governments passed many of the reforms the Chartists had wanted. Chartism was important because it gave working people a way of showing their discontent, and it brought their demands to public notice.

QUESTIONS

1   *Give two reasons why Chartism revived in 1848.*
2   *(a) Why was the government particularly worried at this time?*
    (b) What preparations did they make?
3   *(a) Why do you think O'Connor did not want violence?*
    (b) What does this suggest about his earlier call for physical force?
    (c) Study the illustration: 'The Chartist Meeting on Kennington Common'. Do you think the people there intended using violence?
4   *Study the extracts from* Hansard *carefully, and list four ways in which the Parliamentary Committee criticised the petition.*
5   *(a) Look back over the Six Points of the Charter, and find out how many of them are now law.*
    (b) Do you think Chartism was important? Give reasons for your answer.

ASSIGNMENTS

A. *Write a short essay explaining the main reasons for the growth of Chartism.*
B. *Describe the different ways the Chartists used to attract support, and to try to persuade Parliament to meet their demands.*
C. *Chartism has been described as "hunger politics". Remind yourself of conditions in the country during the three main periods of Chartist activity – 1839, 1842 and 1848 – and then explain why this is a suitable title for the movement.*
D. *Imagine you were present at a Chartist meeting. Write a letter to a friend describing what took place. Include in your letter a description of the audience, the main points raised by the speaker, questions and heckling by the audience, any reaction by the authorities, etc.*
E. *Try to work out why the Chartists failed to get their demands passed at that time. Consider such points as the leadership of the movement; divisions in the movement; changes in the level of support; the attitude of Parliament and the authorities; and any other points you can think of.*

8 Peel, Free Trade and the Corn Laws

The Tory Party and Reform

Until 1832 the Tory Party was thought of as a party which was opposed to any reform. It fought the 1832 Parliamentary Reform Bill tooth and nail (see Chapter 4, pages 57–59), although it was unable to prevent it becoming law, and most Tories were suspicious of any significant changes in the government of Britain.

However, there were some men in the Tory Party who felt it was the government's duty to introduce changes when it could be shown that they were necessary. In the 1820s, William Huskisson had relaxed many of the laws which restricted Britain's trade, and Robert Peel had made the penal law more humane, improved prison conditions and begun Britain's first organised police force in London. (See Chapter 3.) After 1830 Peel became the Tory leader in the House of Commons and tried to change the party's thinking on the question of reform.

Peel's 'Tamworth Manifesto', 1834

> . . . if, by adopting the spirit of the Reform Bill, it be meant that we are to live in a perpetual vortex [whirlwind] of agitation; that public men can only support themselves in public estimation by adopting every popular impression of the day, – by promising the instant redress of anything which anybody may call an abuse, – . . . if this be the spirit of the Reform Bill, I will not undertake to adopt it. But if the spirit of the Reform Bill implies merely a careful review of institutions . . . undertaken in a friendly temper, combining, with the firm maintenance of established rights, the correction of proved abuses and the redress of real grievances, – in that case, I can . . . undertake to act in such a spirit and with such intentions.
>
> ('Tamworth Manifesto', in Mahon and Cardwell, (eds.) *Memoirs of Sir Robert Peel*)

In Peel's 1841–6 government we have already seen that the Tory Party was ready to consider reforms where they were clearly necessary. Conditions in the mines were improved by the Mines Act of 1842, and factory conditions by the Factory Act of 1844. (See Chapter 5.)

Peel and Free Trade

William Huskisson, President of the Board of Trade in the 1820s, had already increased Britain's trade with other countries by abolishing many customs duties and reducing others. Peel continued with this work in the 1840s following the recommendations of the Select Committee on Import Duties in 1840.

Peel's Free Trade measures

Peel's 1842 Budget took the greatest step towards free trade up to that time. Duties were reduced so that the maximum duty on finished manufactured goods was 20 per cent, on part manufactured goods 12 per cent, and on raw materials 5 per cent. In Peel's 1845 Budget, duties were reduced still further, and abolished altogether on over 400 articles. Frederick Engels commented:

> Every obstacle was mercilessly removed. The tariff . . . [was] revolutionised. Everything was made subordinate to one end, but that end of the utmost importance to the manufacturing capitalist: the cheapening of all raw produce, and especially of the means of living of the working class; the reduction of the cost of raw material, and the keeping down . . . of wages. England was to become the 'workshop of the world'; all other countries were to become for England . . . markets for her manufactured goods, supplying her in return with raw materials and food.
>
> (Engels, *The Condition of the Working Class in England*)

Peel realised that the government would lose income by abolishing and reducing so many customs duties, but the aim was that this would be more than made up for by the increase in trade which would result from the free trade measures. However, until trade did start to increase, Peel had to make up for the loss in government income. He stated:

> . . . I consider it more just and more prudent to meet the difficulty at once by proposing a tax upon incomes, than by reviving indirect taxes [i.e. on the goods which people bought], which entail a heavy expense in collecting,

and which cannot be reinforced without greatly disturbing the trade and manufactures of the country. I solve the difficulty by the income tax at the same time that I relieve the consumer by reducing the taxation upon articles of general consumption.

(W.T. Haly *The Opinions of Sir Robert Peel*, 1843)

Income tax (of 2*s* in the pound) had been abolished by Lord Liverpool's Tory Government in 1816, who declared that it had been levied as a temporary measure to raise money during the Napoleonic Wars. Peel now revived this tax at the rate of 7*d* (about 3p) in the pound.

After the free trade measures of 1842–5, only the Corn Laws stood in the way of complete free trade.

QUESTIONS

1   *In the 'Tamworth Manifesto', what did Peel say the Tory Party should stand for, and what did he think it should oppose?*
2   *(a) Make a note of the free trade measures carried out by Peel between 1842 and 1845.*
    (b) What effect would the abolition or reduction of duties have on the cost of imported raw materials?
    (c) Which class did Engels say this was designed to benefit?
    (d) How would working people be affected by the reduction and abolition of duties, according to Engels?
3   *(a) Why did Peel re-introduce income tax in 1842?*
    (b) What advantage did income tax (a direct tax) have over indirect taxes?
    (c) Why would working people prefer an income tax to an increase in indirect taxes?

Peel and the Corn Laws

The traditional Tory view of the Corn Laws

Nearly all the Tory Party were keen supporters of the Corn Laws. As landowners, they believed that agriculture should be protected from foreign competition. When the government proposed to alter the 'Sliding Scale' in 1841 (see page 33), they received this petition:

The humble petition of the undersigned, the Inhabitants of North and South Cadbury, in the county of Somerset, Sheweth,

. . . the proposed alteration of the present Corn Law will be, if carried into effect attended with dangerous consequences to the Nation, deluding the people with the expectation that cheap bread could be obtained without a corresponding lowering of wages . . . we consider it the first duty of the legislature to ensure . . . a certain, regular and sufficient supply of wheat for the consumption of the people, and that the present Corn Law effects that object as near as may be; . . . every security and encouragement must be afforded to home cultivation; . . . it will be most ruinous . . . to place dependence upon foreign countries for the supply of wheat, instead of mainly relying on our native resources . . .

James Bennett, S. Blackall, John Gifford &c. &c. &c.

(Votes and Proceedings of the House of Commons, 1841)

Peel's view in 1841

Peel believed in protection for British agriculture, but not at all costs. When the price of bread rose sharply in 1841 soon after he became Prime Minister, he commented:

> . . . if I could believe that an alteration of the Corn Laws would preclude the risk of such distress . . . I would say at once to the agricultural interest . . . that it would be for the interest, not of the community in general, but especially of the agriculturalists themselves, if, by any sacrifice of theirs, they could prevent the existence of such distress . . . I would earnestly advise a relaxation, nay, if necessary, a repeal of the Corn Laws. But it is because I cannot convince my mind that the Corn Laws are at the bottom of this distress . . . that I am induced to continue my maintenance of them . . .

(Hansard, lix, 413–29, 27 August 1841)

The Anti-Corn Law League

This organisation was formed in 1839 by two wealthy factory owners – Richard Cobden of Manchester and John Bright of Rochdale. Its aim was the total repeal of the Corn Laws.

Cobden against the Corn Laws

. . . He [Cobden] alluded to the food-tax. The people of this country had been petitioning for three years. They were anxious for a total repeal of the food-tax . . . he was also for a total and unconditional repeal of that tax . . . What was this bread tax . . . He had heard that tax called a multitude of names. Some designated it as 'protection'; but it was a tax after all, and he would call it nothing else. The bread-tax was levied principally on the working classes. He called the attention of the House to the working of the bread-tax. The effect was this – it compelled the working classes to pay 40 per cent more, that is, a higher price than they should pay if there was a free trade in corn.

(*Hansard*, lix, 235–42, 25 August, 1841)

Cobden's arguments

In the first place, we want free trade in corn, because we think it just; . . . We do not seek free trade in corn primarily for the purpose of purchasing it at a cheaper money rate; we require it at the natural price of the world's market, whether it becomes dearer . . . or whether it is cheaper, it matters not to us, provided the people of this country have it at its natural price, and every source of supply is freely opened . . .

Neither do we believe it will injure the farm-labourer; we think it will enlarge the market for his labour . . . We do not expect it will injure the land-owner, provided he looks merely to his pecuniary [i.e. money] interest in the matter; . . .

We are satisfied that those landowners who choose to adopt the improvement of their estates, . . . if they will increase the productiveness of their estates . . . then, I say, free trade in corn does not necessarily involve pecuniary injury to the landlords themselves . . .

(From a speech in London on 3 July 1844. Cobden's *Speeches*, 1870, vol. 1, pp. 187–208)

Edward Cardwell further explained why he thought repeal of the Corn Laws would not harm landowners:

A man with 30/- a week would consume more bread, butter, beef, mutton and other agricultural produce, than a man with 8/- or even 16/- and, when the consumption of agricultural produce was thus increased, the profits of the farmer would be increased likewise, and the condition of the agricultural labourer would be proportionately bettered.

(Edward Cardwell, speaking in the House of Commons, February 1846; in Elie Halèvy, *History of the English People in the Nineteenth Century*, vol. 4., Benn, 1961)

The Anti-Corn Law League was supported by other wealthy manufacturers like Cobden and Bright, so it had large funds with which to carry out its campaign for repeal. Alexander Somerville, a journalist and sympathiser with the League, described a visit to its headquarters at Newall's Buildings in Manchester.

The organisation of the League's campaign (1)

Having a day to spend in Manchester, . . . I determined to get a peep, if possible, at that extraordinary body the Anti-Corn Law League . . .

Here we have a large room, . . . for a number of men, who meet in the evenings, and who are called the 'Manchester Committee' . . .

During the day this room is occupied by those who keep the accounts . . . A professional accountant is retained for this department . . .

Passing from this room we come to another, from which all the correspondence is issued. From this office letters to the amount of several thousand a-day go forth to all parts of the kingdom. While here, I saw letters addressed to all the foreign ambassadors, and all the mayors and provosts of corporate towns in the United Kingdom . . . Into this office copies of all the parliamentary registries of the kingdom are kept, so that any elector's name and residence is at once found, and, if necessary, such elector is communicated with by letter or parcel of tracts . . .

In another large room on this floor is the packing department. Here, several men are at work making up bales of tracts . . . and despatching them to all parts of the kingdom for distribution amongst the electors. From sixty to seventy of these bales are sent off in a week, that is, from three to three and a half tons of arguments against the Corn Laws!

. . . in addition to the printing and issuing of tracts here, the League has several other printers at work in this and other towns of the Kingdom.
(A. Somerville, *The Whistler at the Plough*, 1852, pp. 79–82)

The Organisation of the League's Campaign (2)

. . . the League opened books for the registration of land and houses for sale, surveyed the property, prepared the conveyancing deeds, and, in short, left the purchaser nothing to do but to choose his property, pay for it, and take possession . . .'

(Martineau, *History of Thirty Years' Peace*, vol II, p. 615)

Cobden described Bright's plan to buy land in a letter to George Wilson:

. . . Bright & I have been talking over the idea of the Leaguers buying a landed estate in Bucks, or elsewhere with a view to create say 1000 county votes. He thinks that if this purpose were announced in my speech on Thursday, *not* as a scheme for creating votes but strictly with a view to establish a model farm . . . to prove our faith in our principles that the soil is as capable of as great a profitable development as manufactures, that it would strike everybody & create a deal of talk.

(An undated letter in the Wilson Papers, Central Reference Library, Manchester)

The organisation of the League's campaign (3)

[Cobden's description of a conference of 650 ministers in Manchester in 1841:]

There were at that meeting members of the established church, of the Church of Rome, Independents, Baptists, members of the Church of Scotland, and of the Secession Church, Methodists, and, indeed, ministers of every other denomination, . . . Those revered Gentlemen had prepared and signed a petition, in which they prayed for the removal of those laws – laws which, they stated, violated the Scriptures, . . . and he [Cobden] would remind honourable Gentlemen that, besides these 650 ministers, there were 1500 others, from whom letters had been received, offering up their prayers in their several localities to incline the will of Him who ruled princes and potentates to turn your hearts to justice and mercy.

(Cobden's maiden speech, 25 August, 1841 *Hansard*, lix., 235–242)

QUESTIONS

1   What reason is given by the people of North and South Cadbury for the maintenance of the Corn Laws?

2   (a) How did Peel's opinion about the Corn Laws differ from that of most people in the Tory Party?
(b) Why then did Peel not oppose the Corn Laws in 1841, when bread prices were high, and there was much distress in Britain?

3   (a) Why did Cobden call the Corn Laws a 'bread-tax'?
(b) Who suffered most from paying this tax, according to Cobden?
(c) Even if repeal of the Corn Laws did not lead to cheaper bread, how else did he (Cobden) say that the people of Britain would benefit?
(d) How did Cobden and Edward Cardwell say that repeal would affect:
(i) landowners?   (ii) farm labourers?

PAPA COBDEN TAKING MASTER ROBERT A FREE TRADE WALK.

PAPA COBDEN – 'Come along, MASTER ROBERT, do step out.'

MASTER ROBERT – 'That's all very well, but you know I cannot go so fast as you do.'

(*e*) *Look back to the petition from the people of North and South Cadbury. Which selfish reason do they hint at which factory owners such as Cobden and Bright might have had for supporting repeal of the Corn Laws?*

4   (*a*) *What evidence is there in Alexander Somerville's description of Newall's Buildings that: (i) the Anti-Corn Law League was carrying out a very large-scale campaign?   (ii) the campaign was very carefully organised?*
(*b*) *Who were supplied with Anti-Corn Law League literature?*
(*c*) *Why was it possible for the League to carry out such an expensive, nation-wide campaign?*

5   (*a*) *What was the real purpose of the purchase of land by the League?*
(*b*) *Why did the League want 'county votes'?*
(*c*) *What was the impression they were trying to give to landowners?*

6   (*a*) *What reason did Cobden give for the ministers' opposition to the Corn Laws?*
(*b*) *Why do you think the Anti-Corn Law League organised a meeting of ministers from so many different churches?*

Peel's change of mind over the Corn Laws

Cobden was elected M.P. for Stockport in 1841, and Bright also entered Parliament as M.P. for Durham in 1843. It was now possible to present their arguments directly to Peel, and they managed to convince him that repeal of the Corn Laws would be in Britain's best interests. However, Peel could not try to introduce a Bill for repeal as quickly as Cobden and Bright would have liked. But events in Ireland were soon to bring Peel to a decision:

The situation in Ireland

Most Irish workers earned their living as tenant farmers or agricultural labourers. There was only a little industry in the northern part of the country. The landlords were mainly Anglo-Irish, and often did not live on their estates in Ireland. Many took little interest in improving the land they owned with the new farming methods which were being widely used in the rest of Britain. As a result, agriculture was backward, and most people working on the land were very poor.

Farming and Poverty
The great mass of the population consists of small tenants who occupy without partitions, and a potato patch just large enough to supply them most scantily with potatoes through the winter. In consequence of the great com-

petition which prevails amongst these small tenants, the rent has reached an unheard-of height, double, treble and even quadruple that paid in England. For every agricultural labourer seeks to become a tenant-farmer, and . . . the division of the land has gone so far . . .

The Irish people is thus held in crushing poverty . . . These people live in the most wretched clay huts, scarcely good enough for cattle-pens . . . they have potatoes half enough for thirty weeks in the year, and the rest nothing. When the time comes in the Spring when this provision reaches its end, . . . wife and children go forth to beg, . . . Meanwhile the husband . . . goes in search of work either in Ireland or England, and returns at the potato harvest to his family. This is the condition in which nine-tenths of the Irish country folks live. They are poor as church mice, wear the most wretched rags, and stand upon the lowest plane of intelligence possible in a half-civilised country.

(Engels, *The Condition of the Working Class in England*)

The Potato Crop
This root, as compared with other food stuffs grown in this climate, supplied the largest amount of human food on the smallest surface. Its peculiar cultivation enabled the occupier of land to plant it in the wettest soils.

The indolent occupier, therefore, passed his winter inactively, consuming this food which he preferred to all others, and neglecting to prepare his land permanently for more profitable crops, of which he had heard little, and cared less. Enjoying all the while the pleasing delusion, that, as sure as the spring came round, any portion he might select of his farm would be ready to receive his favourite root, and to furnish a certain supply of food for his numerous and increasing family.

(Devon Report, *Digest of Evidence on Occupation of Land in Ireland*, 1847, Pt. 1, 14–16)

The population of Ireland was increasing rapidly. In 1821, it was 6.8 million; in 1841, it was 8.2 million. This led to competition for the available land, which in turn led tenants to sub-let their land, because of the great demand.

Non-improvement of land by the landowner
With this constant and irresistible tendency to subdivide land, it often happens that the landlord, at the expiration of a lease, finds thirty or forty tenants, and as many mud cabins, instead of the one tenant to whom the

farm was originally let. What is a landlord . . . to do? Either he must surrender to the evil . . . or he must set about clearing his estate . . . Now there are only two ways in which a landlord can set about clearing the estate; he may buy out tenants . . . or he may forcibly eject them, and throw down their cabins . . .
(George Cornewall Lewis, *On Local Disturbances in Ireland, and on the Irish Church Question*, London, 1836, pp. 320–1)

Non-improvement by the tenant-farmer
. . . the occupiers not having any certainty of receiving compensation if removed immediately after having effected valuable improvements; and to their not generally having leases, or that security of tenure of their farms which would justify them in expending labour or money in their improvement, as, if they did so, the proprietor would then have the power of immediately increasing the rent . . .
(*The Devon Report, Digest of Evidence on Occupation of Land in Ireland*, 1847, Pt. 1, 14–16)

Widespread poverty and evictions led to acts of violence against landlords.

Crime in the Irish countryside
The attempts of the Irish to save themselves from their present ruin, on the one hand, take the form of crimes. These are the order of the day in the agricultural districts, and are nearly always directed against the most immediate enemies, the landlords' agents, or their obedient servants, the Protestant intruders, whose large farms are made up of the potato patches of hundreds of ejected families. Such crimes are especially frequent in the South and West.
(Engels, *Condition of the Working Class in England*)

The potato blight
Belfast, 18 October 1845
                    Potatoes!
Read – For the sake of the country Read. . . . No man can stop the disease; nor can any man be certain that a single tuber will remain in the island at the end of a few months! In this lies the terrific danger – The RISK is absolutely appalling. *Two thirds* at least of the peasantry have nothing – absolutely NOTHING, to depend upon for existence save the potatoes . . . If their potatoes decay they must die by the Million.
(James Burns to the Duke of Wellington, W.MSS)

The Duke of Wellington, a supporter of the Corn Laws until that time, received this pleading letter in 1845. In that year, potato blight, a fungus disease caused by the wet summer, caused most of the potato crop in Ireland to rot. Since most Irish people depended on potatoes as their main source of food, the danger of famine was obviously very great.

Peel and the end of the Corn Laws

By 1845, Peel had already been convinced by Cobden that repeal of the Corn Laws would benefit most people in Britain; working people would be able to buy cheaper bread when foreign corn could be freely imported, and landowners would also benefit, provided they became more efficient in farming and met the challenge from foreign farmers.

Most of the Tory Party disagreed with Peel. They were landowners who feared that cheap foreign corn entering Britain would lower corn prices and harm British farmers. Peel therefore decided to wait until a General Election. Then he could put his point of view to the voters.

However, the danger of famine in Ireland meant Peel could delay no longer. In a letter to the members of his Cabinet, he stated:

> ... The evil [i.e. the potato blight] *may be* much greater than present reports lead us to anticipate. Potatoes which now appear safe may become infected, and we must not exclude from our consideration ... a great calamity ...
>
> I recommend, therefore, that we should in the first place adopt some such measures as were adopted at former periods of partial scarcity ...
>
> It appears to me that the adoption of these measures, the advance or promise of public money to provide food or employ labour ... will compel the assembling of Parliament before Christmas ...
>
> I cannot disguise from myself that the calling together of Parliament ... will constitute a great crisis, and that it will be dangerous for the government, having assembled Parliament, to resist with all its energies any material modification of the Corn Law.
>
> ... We must make our choice between determined maintenance, modification, and suspension of the existing Corn Law.
>
> In writing the above I have merely considered the question on its own abstract merits, without reference to mere party considerations ... I am fully aware of the gravity of the considerations connected with this part of the question.   ROBERT PEEL.

(Mahon and Cardwell eds., *Memoirs of Sir Robert Peel*, ii, 141–8)

Peel's party was still against repeal. Even the Chancellor of the Exchequer, who had supported Peel's earlier free trade measures, was afraid of the effects of repeal:

> ...In my opinion the party of which you are the head is the only barrier which remains against the revolutionary effects of the Reform Bill. So long as that party remains unbroken, whether in or out of power, it has the means of doing much good, or at least of preventing much evil. But if it be broken in pieces by a destruction of confidence in its leaders (and I cannot but think that an abandonment of the Corn Law would produce that result), I see nothing before us but the exasperation of class animosities, a struggle for pre-eminence, and the ultimate triumph of unrestrained democracy.
>
> Believe me &c.,
HENRY GOULBURN.
>
> (Mahon and Cardwell eds., '*Memoirs of Sir Robert Peel*,' ii, 201–4)

Most of the Tory Party were shocked that Peel should even think of abolishing the Corn Laws. Benjamin Disraeli, a rising young Tory at that time, said of Peel and Peel's supporters in the Cabinet:

> Gentlemen...profess doctrines contrary to those of the new economists. They place themselves at the head of [the Tory] party, and clamber into power...We trusted to one who at this moment governs England...Suddenly, the announcement...another change, which only a few months before [Peel] had described as a 'social revolution'. And how was this announcement made? It was announced through the columns [of *The Times*].
> (*Hansard* 3, LXXXVI, 665–79)

Peel realised that the repeal of the Corn Laws would not be an immediate solution to the famine in Ireland. Government money was therefore made available to enlarge the schemes of public works already being organised by the Irish Board of Works since 1831. The unemployed and starving were offered jobs in road repairs and in drainage and sewage schemes. Food bought abroad was also imported into Ireland by the British Government.

Temporary Measures (1)
Whether wages were at a low rate or at a high rate made no difference. In many districts only 6*d*. or 8*d*. (2½p–3p) a day was offered; nevertheless, whatever the rate, the prospect of wages paid into the labourers' hand in

coin was irresistible, and holdings were left uncultivated and farming operations abandoned as eager crowds besieged the relief committee rooms for employment . . .
(Cecil Woodham-Smith, *The Great Hunger*, Hamish Hamilton, p. 83)

Temporary Measures (2)
Eight thousand tons of Indian Corn and meal was the quantity, by no means excessive, ultimately imported by the British Government into Ireland, . . . on the 13th day (May, 1846) Coffin (Senior Officer of the Commissariat at Limerick) had written that opening should be postponed until further supplies had come in.

Nevertheless, the opening (of depots where Indian corn could be bought) took place. Routh (the Senior Officer of the Commissariat in Dublin) directed Coffin to restrict supplies as far as possible . . .

A rush followed; at about 1d. a pound the Government Indian corn was by far the cheapest food available, and depots everywhere were besieged. At Limerick, Coffin was writing two or three letters a day to relief committees to explain why demands could not be met . . . These and similar letters were received by the committees throughout Ireland with angry indignation.
(Woodham-Smith, *The Great Hunger*, p. 84)

Repeal at last

Peel knew that most of his party would not support a Bill to repeal the Corn Laws. His government therefore resigned. It was now up to the opposition party, the Whigs, led by Lord John Russell, to try to form a government which could successfully carry through repeal. When Russell was unable to do this, Peel and the Tories came back into power in January, 1846. Peel now introduced a Bill for repeal, and tried to persuade a majority of M.P.s, both Tories and Whigs, with the following arguments:

15 May 1846
. . . Sir, I do not rest my support of this Bill merely on the temporary ground of scarcity in Ireland . . . but I believe that scarcity left no alternative to us but to undertake the consideration of this question . . . I think that a permanent adjustment of the question is not only imperative, but the best policy for all concerned . . . we wish to elevate in . . . society that great class which gains its support by manual labour . . . The mere interests of the landlords –
. . . important as they are, are subordinate to the great question – what is

calculated to increase the comforts, to improve the condition, ... of the millions who subsist by manual labour, whether they are engaged in manufactures or in agriculture? I wish to convince them that our object has been so to apportion taxation, ... and transfer it, so far as is consistent with the public good, to those who are better enabled to bear it.

(*Speeches of Sir Robert Peel*, 1853, iv. 689–96)

After a great struggle lasting nearly six months, both the House of Commons and the House of Lords voted in favour of the Bill. Even the opposition of Disraeli and other 'protectionists' in both parties could not prevent it becoming law in June, 1846.

An outbreak of violence in Ireland made it necessary for Peel's government to introduce a Coercion Bill to try to control the violence. His enemies in Parliament had not forgiven him for abolishing the Corn Laws, and they now voted to defeat the Coercion Bill and cause Peel to resign as Prime Minister and Tory Party leader.

The Effects of Repeal

Peel's Resignation Speech, 1846
In relinquishing power ... it may be that I shall leave a name sometime remembered with expressions of goodwill in the abodes of those whose lot it is to labour ... when they shall recruit their strength with abundant and untaxed food, the sweeter because it is no longer leavened by a sense of injustice.

(*Speeches of Sir Robert Peel*, 1853, iv. 716–17)

The Public's Opinion of Peel
He fell from official power into the arms of the people, whose enthusiastic plaudits accompanied him, on the evening of his resignation of office, to his residence in Whitehall Gardens ... They felt instinctively that he must be pure and single minded ... for what had he, raised aloft upon the bucklers of a powerful and wealthy party, to gain from stooping from that dazzling height, to raise up the humble and lowly from the mire into which ignorant and partial legislation had so long trampled them.

(Obituary article on Sir Robert Peel; in Chambers, *Papers for the People* vol. iv. (It was a popular mass periodical of the time.))

PUNCH'S MONUMENT TO PEEL.

British Agriculture

It is now commonplace . . . that farmers feared that repeal of the corn laws would ruin English agriculture, but that on the contrary, the repeal ushered in the period of greatest prosperity the English farmers enjoyed throughout the century. In the first few years after the repeal, however, it was not so clear . . . as it has subsequently become . . . that agriculture was not heading for ruin. Though wheat prices were higher in the year following repeal than they had been for many years, they fell persistently for the next three years, while imports of grain more than doubled between 1846 and 1849. Moreover . . . grain farmers observed that . . . wheat prices in the late 1840's stood at about the same level three-quarters of a century before, butter and wool had doubled their prices, and meat prices had risen by seventy per cent.

(James Caird, *English Agriculture in 1850–1*, 1852, p. 499)

Ireland

Mr. Richard Inglis, a Commissariat officer, was ordered to Skibbereen on about December 17, and horrified by what he saw he sent a statement to Mr. Hewetson, the Senior Commissariat officer at Limerick . . . As Mr. Inglis arrived in Skibbereen he saw three dead bodies lying in the street, and he buried them with the help of the constabulary. Deaths were occurring daily; 197 persons had died in the workhouse since November 5, and nearly 100 bodies had been found dead in the lanes or in derelict cabins . . . Major Parker, Relief Inspector of the Board of Works, estimated that about 200 people had died in Skibbereen during the last few weeks . . . he wrote on December 21 . . . 'nothing can exceed the deplorable state of this place.'

(Woodham-Smith, *The Great Hunger*, p. 163)

The repeal of the Corn Laws came too late to help Ireland, as the horrifying description above makes clear. The potato crop failed again in 1846, and also in 1848. Between 1845 and 1850, Ireland's population of about 8 million was reduced by starvation and by emigration to about 6 million.

QUESTIONS

1 (a) *'Do step out.' What does Cobden mean by saying this to Peel in the* Punch *cartoon (page 126)?*
(b) *As Tory leader, why could Peel not 'step out' and 'go as fast' as Cobden would have liked?*

2   (a) *Why did most Irish tenant-farmers rent such a small area of land?*
    (b) *Find as many reasons as you can why potatoes were preferred to other crops in Ireland. What danger is there in relying only on one crop?*
    (c) *Why did many Irish landowners find it necessary to evict tenant-farmers from their estates?*
    (d) *Why did the tenant-farmers not make the effort to improve their holdings of land?*
    (e) *Of what 'terrific danger' did James Burns warn the Duke of Wellington in 1845?*
3   (a) *Why did Peel intend to wait for a General Election before announcing his opposition to the Corn Laws?*
    (b) *What caused him to change his mind and introduce a Bill for repeal* before *an election?*
    (c) (i) *'I cannot disguise from myself . . . that it will be dangerous for the government.' What danger to the Tory Government did Peel anticipate if he tried to have the Corn Laws repealed?*   (ii) *What did Henry Goulburn, Peel's Chancellor of the Exchequer, say would happen to the Tory Party if Peel went ahead with his proposal for repeal?*   (iii) *What did Disraeli and most of the Tory Party think of Peel's proposal?*
4   (a) *What work did Peel offer the Irish unemployed?*
    (b) *How do we know that the Irish were desperate to accept such work?*
    (c) *What unintended harmful effects did this measure have?*
5   (a) *What substitute did Peel offer the Irish for potatoes?*
    (b) *How can you tell that the supply of this food was inadequate?*
6   *What reasons, apart from the Irish famine, did Peel put forward for the repeal of the Corn Laws?*

ASSIGNMENTS

The Tory Party and Reform
As a supporter of Peel in the Tory Party, write a short speech saying why you agree with Peel that the Tory Party should not oppose all *reform.*

Peel, Free Trade and the Corn Laws
A. *Design an Anti-Corn Law League poster setting out the arguments for free trade in corn, and calling on public support for repeal of the Corn Laws.*
B. *Report on a conversation between a manufacturer and a landowner, setting out the arguments of the former in favour of free trade, and those of the latter against it.*

C. *Imagine you were a working person in 1846 who has just heard the news of Peel's resignation. Write a letter to your local newspaper in praise of Peel's efforts on your behalf, in the face of opposition from most of his party.*

D. *Imagine you were a Member of Parliament in the late 1840s. Write a speech you intend to make, showing your concern over the effect of repeal of the Corn Laws on British agriculture, and at the continuing situation in Ireland, despite repeal and the other measures taken by Peel to help Ireland.*

9 Transport Improvements

Roads

In Chapter 1 we dealt with the great expansion in British industry which became known as the Industrial Revolution. A good transport system was essential for these changes to take place. Raw materials had to be brought to factories, and finished goods sent to market, as cheaply as possible; food had to be brought daily to the growing towns and cities; business contracts, orders, letters and news had to be distributed; and, not least, people had to be able to travel in safety, comfort and at reasonable cost. We should not be surprised therefore to find that the industrial revolution was accompanied by a transport revolution.

In the eighteenth and early nineteenth centuries this revolution concerned roads and canals; by 1851 these modes of transport had been overtaken by the railways. Up to the mid-eighteenth century, the cheapest and easiest way of moving goods was by sea and river. Thus, as late as 1775, the Horsehay Iron Company sent its goods on a river and sea voyage of over 640 km from Shropshire round the Welsh coast to Chester – a distance of only 60 km overland! The reason for such a detour is not difficult to find, as Arthur Young found when he visited neighbouring Lancashire five years earlier:

> From Preston to Wigan, I know not in the whole range of the language, terms sufficiently expressive to describe this infernal road . . . let me most seriously caution all travellers, who may accidentally purpose to travel this terrible country, to avoid it as they would the devil; for a thousand to one but they break their necks or their limbs by overthrows or by breakings down. They will meet here with rutts, which I actually measured four feet deep, and floating with mud only from a wet summer; what, therefore, must it be after a winter? The only mending it receives is the tumbling in some loose stones,

which serve no other purpose but jolting a carriage in the most intolerable manner.
(Arthur Young, *A Six Months Tour through the North of England*, 1771, Vol. IV. p. 430–1)

In 1782 a German traveller described his journey by coach from Leicester to London, travelling on top:

> ...the moment we set off, I fancied that I saw certain death await me. All I could do, was to take still faster [tighter] hold of the handle, and to be more and more careful to preserve my balance.
> The machine now rolled along with prodigious rapidity, over the stones through the town, and every moment we seemed to fly in the air; so it was almost a miracle that we still stuck to the coach, and did not fall.
> (*Travels of Carl Philipp Moritz in England in 1782*, p. 211–2; in T. Charles-Edwards and Brian Richardson, *They Saw It Happen, 1689–1897*, pp. 218–9)

Turnpike Trusts

There had been a gradual improvement in the state of many roads during the eighteenth century, however. This was due to the establishment of private companies called Turnpike Trusts. These were established by Act of Parliament and given permission to charge tolls (such as those shown on page 140) over a specified stretch of road. The money collected was to be used for the repair and improvement of the road. The first Turnpike Act was passed in 1706; between 1750 and 1790, 1600 were passed.

Turnpikes were not supervised by any central authority, so the standard of the roads varied. Many people claimed that most of the money was used to line the officials' pockets instead of paying for better roads. One of the most serious problems was the shortage of skilled engineers.

The Great Road-builders – Telford and Macadam

In the nineteenth century, the methods of Thomas Telford and John Loudon Macadam achieved widespread importance.

Telford came from Dumfries and made his name by his work in the Highlands of Scotland where he was responsible for the building of over 1600 km of road, as well as the Caledonian Canal. In 1815 at the request of the Post Office he started work on the London-to-Holyhead road. When it was completed in 1830, the

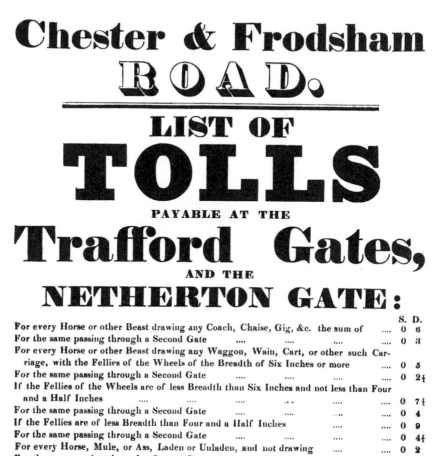

Chester & Frodsham
ROAD.

LIST OF
TOLLS

PAYABLE AT THE

Trafford Gates,
AND THE
NETHERTON GATE:

	S.	D.
For every Horse or other Beast drawing any Coach, Chaise, Gig, &c. the sum of	0	6
For the same passing through a Second Gate	0	3
For every Horse or other Beast drawing any Waggon, Wain, Cart, or other such Carriage, with the Fellies of the Wheels of the Breadth of Six Inches or more	0	5
For the same passing through a Second Gate	0	2¼
If the Fellies of the Wheels are of less Breadth than Six Inches and not less than Four and a Half Inches	0	7¼
For the same passing through a Second Gate	0	4
If the Fellies are of less Breadth than Four and a Half Inches	0	9
For the same passing through a Second Gate	0	4¼
For every Horse, Mule, or Ass, Laden or Unladen, and not drawing	0	2
For the same passing through a Second Gate	0	1
For every Score of Oxen or neat Cattle	1	0
For the same passing through a Second Gate	0	6
For every Score of Pigs, Sheep, Lambs, &c.	0	10
For the same passing through a Second Gate	0	5
For every Waggon, Cart, or such like Carriage, having the Nails of the Tires of the Wheels projecting more than One Quarter of an Inch from the surface of such Tires for each time of passing through any of the above Gates	10	0

Toll to be taken at One Gate only on the Ashton Lane Road.

No exemption from Toll allowed for Manure, Dung, Compost, or Implements of Husbandry, if the Nails of the Wheels project more than a Quarter of an Inch above the Tire or Tires of the Wheels.

A Table of Tolls

482 km road was the finest in country, with its most outstanding feature the Menai suspension bridge linking the Isle of Anglesey to the Welsh mainland.

Telford was most particular about the design of his roads:

> The plan upon which Telford proceeds in road-making is this: first to level and drain: then, like the Romans, to lay a solid pavement of large stones, the broad end downwards, as close as they can be set, the points are then broken off, and a layer of stones, broken to about the size of walnuts, laid over them, so that the whole are bound together; over all a little gravel if it be at hand, but this is not essential.
>
> (R. Southey, *Journal of a Tour in Scotland in 1819*, 1929, p. 54)

Telford's roads were made to last, but this made them expensive, so many hard-pressed Turnpike Trusts preferred the quicker and cheaper methods of Macadam:

> It does not matter if the soil be clay, sand, morass, or bog; I should not care whether the substratum was soft or hard; I should prefer a soft one to a hard one. I never put large stones on the bottom of a road; I would not put a large stone in any part of it.
>
> (J.L. Macadam, *Evidence on Highways of the Kingdom*, 1819)

> The size of stone used on a road must be in due proportion to the space occupied by a wheel of ordinary dimensions on a smooth level surface. The point of contact will be found to be, longitudinally, about an inch, and every piece of stone put into a road, which exceeds an inch in any of its dimensions, is mischievous.
>
> (J.L. Macadam, *Remarks on the Present System of Road-Making*, 1816, p. 35)

Macadam believed that Trusts should join together to produce long stretches of good road. He persuaded Parliament to combine all the Trusts in the London area, and he became Surveyor-General there in 1825.

By 1830, nearly all the main towns of Britain were linked by decent roads, although many local roads were still in a bad state. The result of these improvements was clear:

> The first mail-coach from London to Glasgow arrived at the Saracen's Head on Monday the 7th of July 1788. At that period the mail went by Leeds, a distance of 405 miles [about 650 km] and arrived in 65 hours, travelling at nearly 6½ miles [10 km] in the hour. In 1835 the mail goes by Weatherby, a

distance of 395 miles [about 635 km], and arrives in 41¾ hours. The speed from Carlisle to Glasgow is at the rate of 11 miles [18 km] an hour.

On the 10th of January 1799, Mr John Gardner of the Buck's Head, Glasgow, started a coach to Edinburgh with four horses, which performed the journey of 42 miles [67 km] in 6 hours. The time now occupied on the road by stage-coaches is about 4½ hours.

(*New Statistical Account of Scotland*, 1845, vol VI)

For a short time, the stage-coach reigned supreme. Companies raced each other, offered lower fares and special excursions as they competed for custom. But the great days of coaching were to prove short-lived, as competition developed which was to threaten almost every coaching company – the railway train. The battle was a short one and stage-coaches were relegated to a secondary role of serving stations and areas where the railways did not bother to penetrate.

QUESTIONS

1   Why does an industrial country need a good transport system?
2   Suggest as many reasons as you can to explain why water transport was preferred for moving goods in the eighteenth century.
3   Study the Table of Tolls, then answer these questions:
   (a) How much would be paid by a coach drawn by: (i) 2 horses (ii) 4 horses, at its first gate? Why should the 2 coaches pay different tolls?
   (b) How much would a horse and cart with (i) 8-inch wheel fellies [rims]
   (ii) 4-inch wheel fellies, pay at the second gate?
   (c) Why should these two carts pay different tolls? Do you think it was fair – or sensible?
   (d) Vehicles engaged in which occupation would normally be exempt from payment – if they were properly maintained?
4   What drawbacks did turnpikes suffer from?
5   Draw a cross-section of a road built by (a) Telford; (b) Macadam.
6   Write down the ways in which a journey by coach on a turnpike would be different from that endured by Carl Philipp Moritz (described on p. 139).

ASSIGNMENT

Imagine you overheard a conversation between Thomas Telford and John L. Macadam. Each was defending his own design of road and criticising that built by the other. Write down what might have been said.

Canals

The improvement of the roads meant that people could travel easily and cheaply and a proper mail system could be established. These things were important, but industrialisation required the movement of heavy and bulky goods such as coal, iron-ore and raw cotton. Transporting these by cart or pack-horse was difficult and expensive. It was to fill this need that canal-building started in the last 30 years of the eighteenth century. Previously ships had made use of the many navigable rivers of Britain, but these had problems – flood and drought, winding courses and silt. A navigation canal could avoid those problems, and could also be built where it was wanted most.

James Brindley's Work

The first important canal in Britain was built by James Brindley for the Duke of Bridgewater. The Bridgewater canal ran from the Duke's coal mines at Worsley to Manchester; it was later extended to the port of Liverpool. The results were cheap coal for Manchester; a huge reduction in freight costs for the Manchester cotton masters; and later £70 000 a year profit for the Duke. The canal proved to be one of the wonders of its age:

At Barton bridge he [Brindley] has erected a navigable canal in the air; for it

The Barton Aqueduct over the River Irwell

is as high as the tops of the trees. Whilst I was surveying it with a mixture of wonder and delight, four barges passed me in the space of about three minutes, two of them being chained together, and dragged by two horses, who went on the terras of the canal, whereon, I must own, I durst hardly venture to walk as I almost trembled to behold the large river Irwell underneath me, across which this navigation is carried by a bridge ...
(*Annual Register*, 1763)

Brindley was responsible for about 580 km of canals in the industrial areas of England. After his death, Telford became the foremost canal builder in the country. By the 1820s, a network of canals covered most of England, and to a lesser extent, Wales and Central Scotland. A French visitor was amazed at the achievement which:

within the short space of half a century [had joined up] opposite seas; river-basins separated by numberless chains of hills and mountains; opulent ports; industrious towns; fertile plains; and inexhaustible mines – a system more than 1000 leagues [a league = 5 km] in length ...   ·
(Baron Dupin, *The Commercial Power of Great Britain* (1825), II, p. 341; in J.H. Clapham, *An Economic History of Modern Britain*, 'The Early Railway Age, 1820–1850', p. 75)

Although the canals were mainly designed to serve industry, other groups benefited from them as well:

Coal is the chief article carried upon the [Monkland] Canal; there has latterly been some iron, from the Iron-Works at Calder and Cleland, brought along it, and as the country is favourable for works of this description, the quantity of this article is expected to increase. The only return freight, hitherto, from Glasgow has been manure and lime, neither of them to great amount, but regularly increasing with the extension of agricultural improvement ...
(James Cleland, *Abridgement of the Annals of Glasgow*, 1817, p. 385–6)

The cottage, instead of being covered with miserable thatch, is now secured with a substantial covering of tiles or slates, brought from the distant hills of Wales or Cumberland. The fields, which before were barren, are now drained, and, by the assistance of manure, conveyed on the canal toll-free, are cloathed with a beautiful verdure [greeness]. Places which rarely knew the use of coal are plentifully supplied with that essential article upon reasonable terms: and what is of still greater public utility, the monopolizers of corn are prevented from exercising their infamous trade.

(Thomas Pennant, *The Journey from Chester to London*, 1779)

Another unexpected cargo carried by some canals was people! The Forth and Clyde canal was one of the most successful; in 1815, 85 000 passengers were carried, and the distance of 40 km from Glasgow to Falkirk was covered in 3½ hours.

The canal system of Britain had made the Industrial Revolution possible, by creating a cheap and convenient means of carrying the heavy bulky goods industry needed. But canals did have their problems. Like the Turnpikes there was no overall authority, so the canals and locks of different companies frequently differed in depth and size, often resulting in time-consuming transhipment. They were expensive to build – many owners went bankrupt during construction; others relied on cheap methods and materials, often with disastrous consequences. Finally, canal transport was slow, especially in hilly country when a series of locks had to be negotiated. It was factors such as these which encouraged some industrialists, especially mine-owners, to lay rails for horse-drawn wagons. They were to lead to the decline of the canals, to be replaced by the most revolutionary form of transport during this period – the railways.

QUESTIONS

1 *Make a list of the goods carried by the canals in the extracts. What do most of these goods have in common?*
2 *Suggest reasons why so many people chose to travel by canal.*
3 *How did (a) manufacturers (b) farmers (c) ordinary people, benefit by canals?*
4 *Why do you think people marvelled at Brindley's work?*
5 *What weaknesses did canals suffer from?*

ASSIGNMENT

Imagine you are the Duke of Bridgewater's secretary. You have to write a letter to one of the Duke's fellow landowners, persuading him to build a canal. What arguments would you use?

Trevithick's Catch-Me-Who-Can

Railways

Early Developments

Wooden rails for horse-drawn wagons were used widely around coal-mines in the eighteenth century. The steam engine had also been in use since early in that century. A Cornishman, Richard Trevithick, was first to put the two together. In 1808, he demonstrated his locomotive, which he named 'Catch-Me-Who-Can', in London.

Far from the coalfields, Trevithick did not find the financial support he was seeking in London, and he died years later in poverty. Those who followed, however, did make use of his work. In 1812 a steam locomotive operated in a colliery near Leeds, arousing considerable interest. An observer of this marvel, John Walker, wrote to Mr. Bailey, agent for the Duke of Portland:

> At Leeds they have been daily at work for some time back leading their
> Coals in this way and as their Road is perfectly level their Engines take with

great ease 24, twenty Boll wagons loaded at a time – each wagon weighs with its contents about 3½ Tons, making together an aggregate weight of 84 Tons. When the Machine is lightly loaded it can be propelled at the rate of 10 Miles [16 km] an hour; but when properly loaded is calculated to go at the rate from 3½ to 4 miles [5.5 to 6.5 km] an hour upon a level way . . .

Should the length of the lead from his Lordship's Concerns in Ayrshire be considerable I have no doubt that an immense saving will be made by the adoption of Mr. Blenkinsop's new method . . .
(Charles Brandling's 'Letter Book'; (private collection of P. Burgoyne Johnson) in J. Addy and E.G. Power (eds.), *The Industrial Revolution (Then and There Sourcebook)*)

George Stephenson

The most important figure in the early development of railways was George Stephenson, assisted by his son Robert. Stephenson was responsible for the building of the Stockton to Darlington railway, opened in 1825 and usually regarded as the first modern railway. Its wagons were still pulled by horses on part of the track, and stationary engines were also used, but locomotive power covered the major part. Although originally intended for coal, this line also carried passengers.

The Liverpool – Manchester Line

The breakthrough for railways came with the opening of the Liverpool to Manchester line in 1830. We have already seen how the canal system also had its foundations in this area, but the case for the new means of transport seemed clear:

By the establishment of a rail-way, the inhabitants of Liverpool will be entitled to buy their coals several shillings per ton below the price which they now pay. By opening the collieries to the sea, Liverpool will become one of the greatest shipping ports for coal in the kingdom. A railroad will facilitate [make easier] the conveyance of this indispensable article, together with the agricultural produce, the iron, limestone etc., throughout the whole manufacturing districts of Lancashire . . .
(*Quarterly Review*, (1825) vol. 31, p. 375)

The purpose of the Liverpool to Manchester railway was to provide an alternative and cheaper means of transport than the Bridgewater canal. As might be expected, there was much opposition to the plan:

When the bill went into committee [in Parliament] the opposition was strong and severe . . . Mr. Stephenson was attacked with an undeserved severity; the claims of the land-owner were placed in a prominent position; the loco-motive was laughed at, the speed was denied . . .

Vegetation, it was prophesied, would cease wherever the locomotive pass-ed. The value of land would be lowered by it; the market gardener would be ruined by it . . . Steam would vanish before storm and frost; property would be deteriorated near a station . . . It was erroneous, impracticable, unjust. It was a great and scandalous attack on private property, upon public grounds.
(J. Francis, *A History of the English Railway*, 1851, vol. I, pp. 106–7)

Even after work on the line started, Stephenson, who had been appointed engineer, found that the opponents to the line did not intend to give in easily:

We have had sad work with Lord Derby, Lord Sefton and Bradshaw the Great Canal Proprietor, whose grounds we go through with the projected Railway. Their ground is blockaded on every side to prevent us getting on with the survey. Bradshaw fired guns through his ground in the course of the night to prevent the Surveyors getting on in the dark . . . the Liverpool Rail-way Company are determined to force a Survey if possible. Lord Sefton says we will have a hundred men against us. The Company thinks the Great men have no right to stop a survey.
(Letters of George Stephenson, Liverpool Public Library; in Eric Richards, *The Leviathan of Wealth*, p. 55)

After construction got under way, there were problems of another nature:

No engineer in his senses would go through Chat Moss if he wanted to make a railroad from Liverpool to Manchester . . . In the centre, where this railroad is to cross, it is all pulp from the top to the depth of 34 feet [10 m]; at 34 feet there is a vein of 4 or 6 inches [10 or 15 cm] of clay; below that there are 2 or 3 feet [0.6 or 0.9 m] of quicksand; and the bottom of that is hard clay, which keeps all the water in.
(Evidence to the Parliamentary Committee, quoted in S. Smiles, *The Story of the Life of George Stephenson*, pp. 169–70)

Stephenson eventually surmounted the problem of Chat Moss by floating the line on rafts of heather. Other engineering feats on the line included a tunnel almost

2 km in length on the outskirts of Liverpool, and nearby the Olive Mount Cutting, itself 30 m deep (see below). The line was finally completed by 1829.

QUESTIONS

1   *Why do you think locomotives were first used around the coal mines?*
2   *Why do you think the Manchester-Liverpool area gave birth to the first major canal and the first major railway?*
3   (a) *What reasons were put forward for establishing the railway?*
    (b) *Which sort of people opposed it?*
    (c) *What arguments did they use?*
4   *What difficulties did Stephenson face in building the line? How did he overcome them?*

The engines

Debate now centred on the type of engine to be used. Most directors of the Company favoured a system of stationary engines, but the Stephensons persuaded them to adopt locomotive power. The directors were determined to have the best, so a competition was held. Robert Stephenson's 'Rocket' won the competition easily. (The competitors at these Rainhill Trials are shown opposite.)

Celebration and tragedy

The line was officially opened on 15 September 1830, with the Duke of Wellington, the Prime Minister, and Liverpool MP William Huskisson, among the guests on a special excursion:

> We started on Wednesday last, to the number of about eight hundred people . . . The most intense curiosity and excitement prevailed, and, though the weather was uncertain, enormous masses of densely packed people lined the road, shouting and waving hats and handkerchiefs as we flew by them. What with the sight and sound of these cheering multitudes and the tremendous velocity with which we were borne past them, my spirits rose to the true champagne height, and I never enjoyed anything so much as the first hour of our progress. I had been unluckily separated from my mother in the first distribution of places, but by an exchange of seats which she was enabled to make she rejoined me when I was at the height of my ecstasy, which was considerably damped by finding that she was frightened to death . . .

The journey was to have a tragic outcome:

> . . . A man flew by us, calling out through a speaking-trumpet to stop the engine, for that somebody in the directors' carriage had sustained an injury.

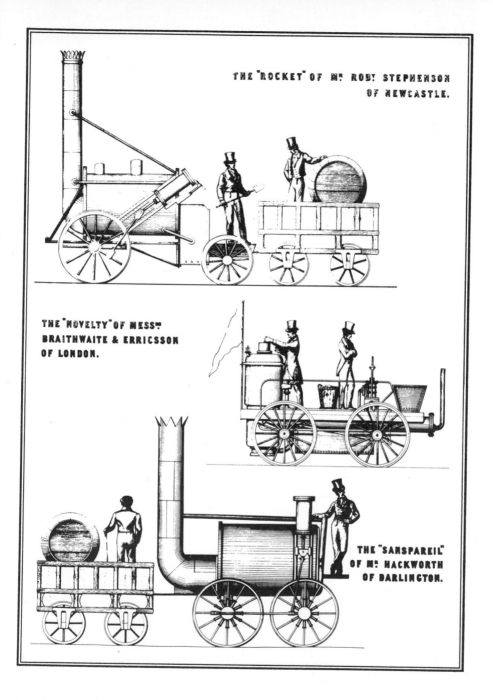

THE "ROCKET" OF M^R. ROB^T. STEPHENSON OF NEWCASTLE.

THE "NOVELTY" OF MESS^RS. BRAITHWAITE & ERRICSSON OF LONDON.

THE "SANSPAREIL" OF M^R. HACKWORTH OF DARLINGTON.

We were all stopped accordingly, and presently a hundred voices were heard exclaiming that Mr. Huskisson was killed . . . the confusion that ensued is indescribable . . . At last . . . I had the following details . . .

The engine had stopped to take in a supply of water, and several of the gentlemen in the directors' carriage had jumped out to look about them . . . an engine on the other line . . . was seen coming down upon them like lightning . . . poor Mr. Huskisson, less active from the effects of age and ill-health . . . completely lost his head, looked helplessly to the right and left, and was instantaneously prostrated by the fatal machine, which dashed down like a thunderbolt upon him, and passed over his leg, smashing and mangling it in the most horrible way . . . Mr. Huskisson was then placed in a carriage . . . with his wife . . . and the engine, having been detached from the directors' carriage, conveyed them to Manchester. So great was the shock produced upon the whole party by this event, that the Duke of Wellington declared his intention not to proceed, but to return immediately to Liverpool. However, upon its being represented to him that the whole population of Manchester had turned out to witness the procession, and that a disappointment might give rise to riots and disturbances, he consented to go on, and gloomily enough the rest of the journey was accomplished.
(Frances Kemble, *Record of a Girlhood*, from a letter dated 20 September 1830)

Poor Huskisson was conveyed from the spot at the astonishing speed of 33¾ miles [about 53 km] an hour, so great was the anxiety of the physicians to get him to the place where amputation (the only chance) could be performed. It was dreadful. Think that out of the hundreds and thousands assembled in the densest masses, he alone should be the sufferer!
(Letter from Currie to Loch, Sutherland Collection, Stafford CRO, quoted in Eric Richards, *The Leviathan of Wealth*, p. 102)

Even in these unfortunate circumstances, the speed of the locomotive was thus publicly demonstrated – but despite the 'Rocket's' efforts, Huskisson died the next day.

Railway expansion

The advantages of the new means of transport were soon clear:

Before the establishment of the Liverpool and Manchester railway, there were twenty-two regular and about seven occasional extra coaches between these places, which, in full, could only carry per day 688 persons. The railway, from its commencement, carried 700 000 persons in eighteen months being an average of 1070 per day. It has not been stopped for a single day. The fare by coach was 10*s*. [50p] inside and 5*s*. [25p] outside – by railway it is 5*s*. inside, and 3*s*. 6*d*. [17½p] outside. The time occupied in making the journey by coach was four hours – by railway it is one hour and three quarters. All the coaches but one have ceased running ... The travelling is cheaper, safer, and easier ... Goods [are] delivered in Manchester the same day they are received in Liverpool. By canal they were never delivered before the third day ... The savings to manufacturers in the neighbourhood of Manchester, in the carriage of cotton alone, has been £20 000 per annum ... Coal pits have been sunk, and manufactories established on the line, giving great employment to the poor ... It is found advantageous for the carriage of milk and garden produce ... A great deal of land on the line has been let for garden ground, at increased rents. Residents on the line find the railway a great convenience, by enabling them to attend to their business in Manchester and Liverpool with ease, at little expense ... The value of land on the line has been considerably enhanced by the operation of the railway ...

(*Annual Register*, 1832, quoted in N. Gash, *The Age of Peel*, pp. 164–5)

QUESTIONS

1 *Why did the Liverpool-Manchester Railway directors hold a competition?*
2 *(a) Why do you think Frances Kemble (who was aged 21) and her mother reacted differently to their train journey?*
(b) Why do you think there were such vast crowds?
(c) How was the tragic accident to Huskisson turned into good publicity for the railway?
3 *List all the advantages claimed for the Liverpool-Manchester Railway.*
4 *What effect do you think the success of this line would have?*

The success of the Liverpool-Manchester railway soon led to the development of other lines. People everywhere believed there were vast profits to be made by investment in new railway lines, and in 1835 a railway mania (madness) gripped the country.

The press supported the mania, the government sanctioned it, the people paid for it. Railways were at once a fashion and a frenzy. England was

mapped out for iron roads. The profits and percentages of the Liverpool and Manchester were largely quoted. The prospects and power of the London and Birmingham were as freely prophesied.
(Francis, *A History of the English Railway*, vol. I, p. 290)

During the mid-forties, a much greater mania developed. Between 1844 and 1846, over 430 proposals for new lines were accepted by Parliament. People made fortunes by buying railway shares; railway companies bought out their smaller competitors. The most important of these railway barons was George Hudson, the 'Railway King', who for a time controlled many of the lines of the Midlands and northern England. Unfortunately it was found that some of Hudson's business deals were fraudulent and he was ruined.

The Stephensons continued to play their part in this expansion. So too, did Isambard Kingdom Brunel, engineer of the Great Western Railway from London to Bristol. Brunel built this track with as few bends as possible, and with gentle gradients, so that high speeds would be possible. As a further aid to safety at speed, he built the line with the rails 7 feet (2.134 m) apart, much wider than the Standard gauge of 4 feet 8½ (1.25 m) inches which all other lines had in common. This difference caused problems when two different lines met.

Building the railways

Although the famous engineers are most remembered, the physical work of building the railways was done by an army of 200 000 men armed with picks and shovels. They were known as 'navvies' since they had originally dug the canals, or 'navigations'. Their lives were extremely hard; an endless round of backbreaking work, drink and sleep. Their work – building embankments, excavating cuttings or boring tunnels – was generally unpleasant and frequently dangerous. Some contractors treated their men well; others regarded them as little more than animals:

> The contractors, being exposed to fierce competition, are tempted to adopt the cheapest method of working, without any close reference to the danger to which the men will be exposed . . . Life is now recklessly sacrificed: needless misery is inflicted; innocent women and children are unnecessarily rendered widows and orphans; and such evils must be not allowed to continue, even though it should be profitable.
> (*Manchester Guardian*, 7 March 1846)

I went round by Eston. We call it the slaughterhouse, you know, because every day nearly there's a accident, and nigh every week, at the farthest, a death. Well, I stood and looked down, and there were the chaps, ever so far below, and the cuttings so narrow. And a lot of stone fell, it was always falling, they were bound to be hurt. There was no room to get away nor mostly no warning. One chap I saw killed while I was there, anyhow he died as soon as they got him home. So, I said, "Good money's all right, but I'd sooner keep my head on," so I never asked to be put on, but came away again.

(In Elizabeth Garnett, *Our Navvies*)

Not all navvies were able to make the same decision. Edwin Chadwick tried to persuade the government to launch an enquiry into the standards of safety amongst the navvies, and he compared the casualties on the Woodhead Tunnel with those in the major battles of the Napoleonic War:

Thirty-two killed out of such a body of labourers, and one hundred and forty wounded, besides the sick, nearly equal the proportionate casualties of a campaign or a severe battle. The losses in this one work may be stated as more than three per cent of killed, and fourteen per cent wounded. The deaths (according to the official returns) in the four battles, Talavera, Salamanca, Vittoria and Waterloo, were only 2.11 per cent of privates . . .

(Edwin Chadwick: *Papers Read Before the Statistical Society of Manchester*, 1846; in T. Coleman, *The Railway Navvies*, p. 124)

When life itself was regarded so cheaply, the navvies' life style does not sound so surprising:

They were in a state of utter barbarism. They made their homes where they got their work. Some slept in huts constructed of damp turf, cut from the wet grass, too low to stand upright in; while small sticks, covered in straw, served as rafters. Barns were better places than the best railway labourers' dwellings. Others formed a room of stones without mortar, placed thatch or flags across the roof, and took possession of it with their families, often making it a source of profit by lodging as many of their fellow-workers as they could crowd into it. It mattered not to them that the rain beat through the roof, and that the wind swept through the holes. If they caught a fever they died, if they took an infectious complaint they wandered in the open air, spreading the disease wherever they went. . . . In such places from nine

to fifteen hundred men were crowded for six years. Living like brutes, they were depraved, degraded, and reckless. Drunkeness and dissoluteness of morals prevailed. There were many women, but few wives.
(Francis, *History of the English Railway*, vol. II, pp. 70–72)

QUESTIONS

1   *Why did the railway mania develop?*
2   *Why did Brunel's broad gauge create a problem?*
3   (*a*) *Why, according to the* Manchester Guardian *did many needless deaths occur among navvies?*
     (*b*) *Why was Eston called 'the slaughterhouse'?*
     (*c*) *Summarise Edwin Chadwick's conclusions about the number of casualties.*
     (*d*) *Describe the living conditions of the navvies.*

Railways for All

Railway Mileage open (cumulative)

1831	140 miles	1847	3945 miles
1835	338	1848	5127
1840	1498	1849	6031
1845	2441	1850	6621
1846	3036	1851	6877

By 1851 the basis of Britain's railway network was complete. All the main centres of population had been joined up, although many branch lines were still to be built. A revolution in transport had taken place, with seemingly limitless consequences:

In the grey mists of the morning, in the atmosphere of a hundred conflicting smells, and by the light of faintly burning gas, we see a large portion of the

supply of the great London markets rapidly disgorged [unloaded] by these night trains: fish, flesh and food, Aylesbury butter and dairy-fed pork, apples, cabbages and cucumbers, alarming supplies of cats' meat, cart loads of water cresses, and we know not what else, for the daily consumption of the metropolis. No sooner do these disappear than at ten minutes' interval arrive other trains with Manchester packs and bales, Liverpool cotton, American provisions, Worcester gloves, Kidderminster carpets, Birmingham and Staffordshire hardware ... At a later hour of the morning these are followed by other trains with the heaviest class of traffic, stones, bricks, iron girders, iron pipes, ale ... coal, hay, straw, grain, flour and salt ...
(*Railway News*, 1864; in G.R. Hawke: *Railways and Economic Growth in England and Wales 1840–1970*, p. 59)

Robert Stephenson considered the impact the railways had had by 1856:

The cost of these lines has been £86 000 000, equal to one third of the amount of the national debt ... 80 000 000 train miles were run annually on the railways, 5000 engines and 150 000 vehicles composed the working stock ... the engines consumed annually 2 000 000 tons of coal ... 20 000 tons of iron required to be replaced annually; and 26 000 000 sleepers annually perished ... The postal facilities afforded by railways were very great. But for their existence Mr. Rowland Hill's plan [the Penny Post] could

First Class

never have been effectively carried out. Railways afforded the means of carrying bulk, which would have been fatal to the old mail coaches . . . The results of railways were astounding. 90 000 men were employed directly and upwards of 40 000 collaterally [indirectly]; 130 000 men with their wives and families, representing a population of 500 000 souls; so that one in fifty of the entire population of the kingdom might be said to be dependent on railways.

(Robert Stephenson, *Address to the Institution of Civil Engineers*, 1856)

Over six million people visited the Great Exhibition in London in 1851 (see Chapter 10). Many of them would have travelled there on excursions. For most of them it would have been their first railway journey, an unforgettable experience.

. . . I started at five o'clock on Sunday evening, got to Birmingham by half-past five on Monday morning [by coach] and got upon the rail-road by half-past seven. Nothing can be more comfortable than the vehicle in which I was put, a sort of chariot with two places, and there is nothing disagreeable about it but the occasional whiffs of stinking air which it is impossible to exclude altogether. The first sensation is a slight degree of nervousness and a feeling of being run away with, but a sense of security soon supervenes, and the velocity is delightful. Town after town, one park and chateau after another are left behind with the rapid variety of a moving panorama, and the constant bustle . . . of the changes and stoppages made the journey

Second Class

very entertaining . . . Considering the novelty of its establishment, there is very little embarrassment and it certainly renders all other travelling irksome and tedious by comparison.
(*Greville Memoirs*, 18 July 1837)

Most railway lines ran carriages of three different classes. First class was the preserve of the wealthy, most middle-class business travellers would have chosen second class, while the third class 'trucks' offered neither seats nor roof. Complaints about the standard of third class travel led the government to make a rare break in the rule of non-interference:

The Railway Act, 1844
Be it enacted that . . . all passenger Railway Companies . . . shall by means of one train at the least to travel along their railway from one end to the other of each trunk, branch or junction line belonging to them . . . once at the least on every week day, except Christmas Day and Good Friday (such exception not to extend to Scotland) provide for the conveyance of Third Class passengers to and from the terminal and other ordinary passenger stations of the railway . . .

The carriages in which passengers shall be conveyed by such train shall be provided with seats and shall be protected from the weather. The fare or charge shall not exceed one penny for each mile travelled.
(*Statutes at Large*, vol. XXVI, p. 451)

Third Class

The building of the railways of Britain involved one of the greatest human physical efforts. The introduction of these 'Parliamentary Trains' ensured that the class which had sweated to bring them about would be able to afford to use them.

> Now, who have specially benefited by this vast invention?
> The rich, whose horse and carriages carried them in comfort over the known world? – the middle classes to whom stage coaches and mails were an accessible mode of conveyance? – or the poor, whom the cost of locomotion [travel] condemned often to an almost vegetable existence? Clearly the latter. The rail-road is the Magna Carta [charter] of their freedom. How few among the last generation ever stirred beyond their own village? How few among the present will die without visiting London? . . . The number who left Manchester by cheap trips in one week of holiday time last year exceeded 202 000; against 150 000 in 1849, and 116 000 in 1848.
> (*The Economist*, 1851)

QUESTIONS

1 *Which years show the most new railway mileage opened? Why are these not the years of the railway 'mania'?*
2 *Show the impact of the railways by explaining the importance of each of the following:*
   (a) fresh goods (b) industrial goods (c) the manufacture of rails and locomotives (d) manning the railways (e) the Penny Post.
3 *(a) Write down the three main terms of the 1844 Railway Act.*
   (b) Why were the 'Parliamentary' trains important?
4 *How was the writer in* The Economist *able to argue that the poor had benefited most from the railways?*

ASSIGNMENTS

A. *Imagine you were chairing a public meeting to discuss whether or not the Liverpool-Manchester Railway should be built. Write a report of the meeting, describing the people who were present and the arguments they put forward.*
B. *Describe the physical difficulties involved in building the railways, and the part played by engineers and navvies in overcoming these difficulties.*
C. *Imagine you are a reporter covering the opening of the Liverpool-Manchester Railway for your paper. Write your report of the events of that day.*

D. *Write a letter to a friend describing your first rail journey.*

E. *Write a letter to a relative overseas describing the impact railways have made. Include in your letter the effects of cheaper transport of goods; cheaper and more travel; the construction of the railways; the Penny Post, etc.*

Steamships

Steam engines were used to power ships before their use on the railways, but it took the steam ship a much longer time to establish its superiority over the sailing ships.

The first successful use of steam power was in William Symington's *Charlotte Dundas* which made its maiden voyage on the Forth and Clyde canal in 1802. In 1812 Henry Bell started Europe's first passenger service in the Firth of Clyde with his ship, the *Comet*:

> The subscriber [Bell], having at much expense, fitted up a handsome vessel to ply upon the river Clyde from Glasgow, to sail by the power of air, wind and steam, intends that the vessel shall leave the Broomielaw on Tuesdays, Thursdays, and Saturdays about mid-day . . . The terms are for the present fixed at 4*s.* [20p] for the best cabin and 3*s.* [15p] for the second.
> (*Glasgow Chronicle*, 12 August 1812)

With the example of the *Comet* before them, regular services were started in other areas. Steam ships continued to carry sails as well, and it was not until 1838 that the American *Sirius* made the first crossing of the Atlantic by steam alone. It was quickly followed by the first of Isambard Kingdom Brunel's great ships, the *Great Western*. Like other steamships of the time, it was a paddle-steamer; but Brunel's *Great Britain* in 1845 became the first propeller-driven steamer to cross the Atlantic. It was also the first important ship to be built of iron.

Brunel's dream was to provide a direct route from London to New York using his Great Western railway to Bristol. His last ship, the *Great Eastern*, launched in 1858 was the largest ship in the world for over 40 years, but it was not a commercial success.

Even by 1851, the age of the steam ship had not fully arrived. Steam ships did have advantages over their rival sailing ships – they did not have to await a favourable wind, and were faster. On the other hand, much of their available space was taken up by the huge quantities of coal which it was necessary to carry. The development of new, faster sailing ships, the *clippers* of the 1850s, provided an extra challenge. The most famous of the clippers was the *Cutty Sark*, which now lies restored at Greenwich in London.

It was really the opening of the Suez canal in 1869 which finally brought victory to the steam ship, by creating a shorter route to the East. At the same time, 'coaling stations' were established on the main sea routes.

QUESTIONS

1   *What advantages did steam ships have over sailing ships?*
2   *Why did it take steam ships so long to establish their superiority?*

ASSIGNMENT

Write an obituary for Isambard Kingdom Brunel (1806–1859), listing and describing his achievements in railways and steam ships.

10 Britain in 1851

Britain's Population

From the beginning of the nineteenth century, Britain's population grew even faster than it had done in the eighteenth century. Not only did the total population increase, but the population of some towns and areas grew much faster than others.

Total population
(excluding Ireland)

1811 – 12.15 million
1821 – 14.21 million
1831 – 16.37 million
1841 – 18.55 million
1851 – 20.88 million

Population of towns
(in thousands)

	1801	1851
Bradford	13	104
Glasgow	77	329
Liverpool	82	376
Birmingham	71	233
Manchester	70	303
Leeds	53	172
London	957	2362
Bath	33	54
Norwich	36	68
York	17	34

The Census of 1851

The most important result which the inquiry establishes, is the addition in half a century, of *ten millions* of people to the British population. The increase of population in the half of this century nearly equals the increase in all preceding ages; and the addition, in the last *ten* years, of *two millions three hundred thousand* to the inhabitants of these islands, exceeds the increase in the last *fifty* years of the eighteenth century . . .

Two other movements of the population have been going on in the United Kingdom: the immigration of the population of Ireland into Great Britain, and the constant flow of the country population into the towns . . . where the towns engage in a manufacture as one vast undertaking, in which nearly the whole population is concerned; as well as to the County towns, and to London . . .

At the same time, too, that the population of the towns and of the country, have become so equally balanced in number – *ten millions* against *ten millions* – . .

(*Census of Great Britain*, 1851, vol. i, 1852, Report, Section 8, lxxxii – lxxxiv) lxxxiv)

Progress between 1815 and 1851

One reason why Britain's population grew so quickly was the continued expansion of industry, at an even faster pace than before 1815. A foreign visitor gave his impression of these changes:

I visited England for the first time 52 years ago . . . to judge how far and how completely . . . industrial activity had developed, as against that which the Continent could show; and I must confess that the verdict fell entirely in favour of England . . .

Yet nothing very new could be observed there at that period . . . the same things were to be found elsewhere, though not so good . . .

Twenty years later . . . I found great new developments in the above mentioned field. Spinning mills, foundries, potteries . . . steel and file factories, the plating works of Birmingham and Sheffield, the spinning and weaving mills of Manchester, and the cloth manufacture of Leeds, had acquired a size and perfection of which there can be no conception without actually seeing them.

Twelve or thirteen years later, . . . the scale of everything and especially the expansion of London had increased yet more . . .

The already extensive steam navigation, the general installation of gas lighting, Perkins's steam-driven shuttles, Brunel's giant tunnel . . . besides much else of the greatest interest . . . remain in my mind . . . as an ever fascinating picture.

(Johann Conrad Fischer, *Tagebucher* (*Diary*), 1851)

The Reverend Sydney Smith noted many improvements in the same period:

It is of some importance at what period a man is born. A young man, alive at this period, hardly knows to what improvements of human life he has been introduced; and I would bring before his notice the follow-ing . . . changes which have taken place since I first began to breathe . . . Gas was unknown: I groped about the streets of London in all but the utter darkness of a twinkling oil lamp, under the protection of watchmen . . . and exposed to every species of depredation and insult.

I have been nine hours in sailing from Dover to Calais before the inven-tion of steam. It took me nine hours to go from Taunton to Bath, before the invention of rail roads, and I now go in six hours from Taunton to London! In going from Taunton to Bath, I suffered between 10 000 to 12 000 severe contusions before stone-breaking Macadam was born.

I can walk, by the assistance of the police, from one end of London to the other, without molestation; or, if tired, get into a cheap and active cab . . .

. . . The corruptions of Parliament, before Reform, infamous . . . The Poor Laws were gradually sapping the vitals of the country; and, whatever mis-eries I suffered, I had no post to whisk my complaints for a single penny to the remotest corners of the empire; . . .

(*Collected Works of the Reverend Sydney Smith*, Longmans, 1839, 'Modern Changes')

Criticisms of Change

There was no doubt that great improvements had taken place in Britain. The industrial revolution had made the country the 'workshop of the world'. Transport developments such as canals and railways had helped the growth of industry, and had even made it possible for working people to leave the areas where they lived and worked. More and better food was available because of the improvements in agriculture. The right to vote had been given in 1832 to some of the middle class, who were now represented in Parliament.

At the same time, there was a lot to criticise.

Working and living conditions

Parliament had passed laws to improve working conditions in factories and mines, but these had not gone far enough. Hours of work were still too long, and children could still be employed in factories and mines, though not so young as before.

Nothing had yet been done to improve safety or health in factories and mines. The Public Health Act of 1848 had set up the Board of Health, but it had been abolished in 1854, and slum living conditions, over-crowding and disease still existed in the industrial towns. Frederick Engels commented on how the Industrial Revolution had caused suffering to the working people of Britain:

> ...In the circumstances [that is, before the industrial revolution] the workers enjoyed a comfortable, peaceful existence...Their standard of living was much better than that of the factory worker today. They were not forced to work excessive hours...eventually machines robbed them of their livelihood and forced them to seek work [in the towns]. The Industrial Revolution...turned the workers completely into mere machines and deprived them of the last remnants of independent activity...
> (Engels, *The Condition of the Working Class in England*)

Emigration

Emigrants at the agent's office

Although the population of Britain was growing rapidly, many people wanted to leave Britain and settle overseas:

> ...with the increase of the population at home, emigration has proceeded since 1750 to such an extent, as to people large states in America, and...large colonies in all the temperate regions of the world.
> (*Census of Great Britain*, 1851, vol. i. (1852) Report, Section 8, lxxxii–lxxxiv.)

Emigration from the United Kingdom to non-European countries

1820-9	216 000
1830-9	668 000
1840-9	1 495 000

Emigrants at dinner

The right to vote

The Parliamentary Reform Act of 1832 had given the right to vote to a few of the middle class. No working people yet had the vote. Some, like the Chartists, wanted the vote to be given to all adult males. In a speech at Birmingham Town Hall in 1865, John Bright said:

> . . . The Tories, and those Whigs who are like Tories, have an uncomfortable feeling which approaches almost to a shiver . . . They are afraid of the five or six millions of Englishmen, grown-up men who are allowed to marry, to keep house, to rear children, who are expected to earn their living, who pay taxes, who must obey the law, who must be citizens in all honourable conduct – they are afraid of the five or six millions who by the present system of representation are shut out . . . from the commonest rights of citizenship.
>
> But perhaps our friends who oppose us will say . . . 'What we fear is this – the . . . results of this wide extension of the franchise.' I am ready to test it

in any country ... I say, whether you go to South Africa, or to Australia, or to the British North American provinces, or to the States of the American Union, you will find – excluding always those states where slavery injures the state of society – you will find that life and property are as secure, you will find that education is much more extended amongst the people, that there is quite as wide a provision for their religious interests, that the laws are as merciful and just, that taxes are imposed and levied with as great equality, and that millions of your countrymen who are now established in those countries are at least as well off ... as are the people of this country whom they have left behind them.
(James E. Thorold Rogers (ed.), *Speeches by John Bright*, 1869, vol. II, pp. 111–127)

However, most upper-class landowners, and even many people from the middle class, feared the results of extending the right to vote to working people. Robert Lowe, a Liberal M.P., put their point of view:

> ... I would point out that the working classes, under the modest claim to share in electoral power, are really asking for the whole of it ... They who set up such a claim must show they are masters of themselves before they can hope to be masters of others ... they will swamp the less numerous classes.
> (Robert Lowe, *Speeches and Letters on Reform*, 1867, pp. 3–16)

Punch magazine had this to say about working people being 'masters of themselves':

THE INTELLIGENCE OF THE PEOPLE
When there is talk of any Extension of the Suffrage, it is naturally enough usual to inquire how far the Intelligence of the People would justify their being entrusted with the right of voting for Members of Parliament. As far as the amount of intelligence can be gathered from the conduct of the people at public meetings of a political character, we regret to say the account is somewhat beggarly. The late election for the City of London presented a very poor result with reference to the wisdom of the masses, who had nothing better than bellowing and roaring to offer, by way of criticism, on the merits of the respective candidates ... Nothing else was audible during the attempts of LORD JOHN MANNERS to address the multitude, whose

intelligence never reached beyond such a remark as 'Go home', 'It won't do here', or some other observation of about equal profundity.
(*Punch*, vol. XVII, 1849, p. 21)

Government action

From 1815 to 1851, governments had passed more and more laws to try to cure the evils of the time. As we have seen, there had been laws dealing with conditions in factories and mines, public health, the Poor Law, police and prisons, and representation in Parliament. However, Samuel Smiles, a famous author and journalist of the time, spoke for many people who felt that the increase in government activity had gone too far:

> 'Heaven helps those who help themselves' is a well-tried maxim . . . Help from without is often enfeebling in its effects, but help from within invariably invigorates. Whatever is done *for* men or classes, to a certain extent takes away the stimulus and necessity of doing for themselves; and where men are subjected to over-guidance and over-government, the inevitable tendency is to render them comparatively helpless.
> . . . Indeed all experience serves to prove that the worth and strength of a State depend far less upon the form of its institutions than upon the character of its men . . .
> National progress is the sum of individual industry, energy, and uprightness, as national decay is of individual idleness, selfishness, and vice.
> (Samuel Smiles, *Self-Help*, 1859, pp. 1–2)

QUESTIONS

1 (a) In which areas was Britain's population increasing the fastest? (See the 1851 census, and also compare the growth of towns such as Bradford, Glasgow or Manchester, with that of towns such as Bath, Norwich or York.)
(b) In 1851, how much of Britain's population lived in the towns, and how much in the countryside? (ii) What would you expect to happen to the proportion of town dwellers to country dwellers after 1851?
2 (a) In what ways had Britain's industry improved by 1851, according to Johann Conrad Fischer?
(b) In what ways did the Rev. Sydney Smith say: (i) Britain's cities had become safer? (ii) travelling and communications had been improved? (iii) government had been improved?

3   What effect had the Industrial Revolution had on working people, according to
    Frederick Engels?
4   (a) Why do you think so many people wanted to leave Britain at this time?
    (b) To which countries did they emigrate?
5   (a) (i) What arguments did John Bright offer for giving working people the
    right to vote? (ii) How did he show that Britain's government would still pass
    fair and just laws, and even become more effective than before, if working
    people had the vote?
    (b) (i) Who were the 'less numerous classes' referred to by Robert Lowe, and
    what did he mean by saying they would be 'swamped'?
    (ii) Why did Punch *magazine oppose giving working people the right to vote?*
6   If a government passed a great number of laws, what did Samuel Smiles say the
    effect would be on (a) an individual? (b) Britain?

ASSIGNMENTS

A. Write letters exchanged by two friends, one of whom has emigrated from
   Britain in 1815, the other is still living in Britain in 1851. In the emigrant's
   letter, set out his or her reasons for leaving Britain at the time. In the reply by
   the friend in Britain, try to point out the changes since 1815, and offer reasons
   why the emigrant might even wish to return.
B. Do you agree with Samuel Smiles that governments should have passed fewer
   laws between 1815 and 1851? Give reasons for your answer.

The Great Exhibition

A Royal Commission was set up to arrange for an international exhibition, which
eventually opened in Hyde Park in London in 1851. The exhibition was organised
by the Prince Consort, Prince Albert, who described the purpose of the Great
Exhibition in this way:

> Gentlemen – the Exhibition of 1851 is to give a true test and a living picture
> of the point of development at which the whole of mankind has arrived in
> this great task, and a new starting-point from which all nations will be able
> to direct their further exertions.
>
> (From a speech by Prince Albert, at a banquet in 1850; in *Principal
> Speeches and Addresses of H.R.H. the Prince Consort*, 1862 pp. 110–2)

Various schemes for a building to hold the Exhibition were rejected as being too large, too heavy or clumsy. Eventually, Joseph Paxton's design was accepted. This was for a building of iron and glass, and, not surprisingly, *Punch* magazine nicknamed it the 'Crystal Palace'.

The Crystal Palace

The opening

Queen Victoria opened the Exhibition on 1 May 1851.

> There was yesterday witnessed a sight the like of which has never happened before, and which . . . can never be repeated . . . In a building that could easily have accommodated twice as many, twenty-five thousand persons, so it is computed, were arranged in order round the throne of our SOVEREIGN. Around them, amidst them, and over their heads was displayed all that is useful or beautiful in nature or in art. Above them rose a glittering arch more lofty and spacious than the vaults of even our noblest cathedrals. On either side the vista seemed almost boundless . . . all contributed to an effect so grand and yet so natural, that it hardly seemed to be put together by design, or to be the work of human artificers.
> (*The Times*, 2 May 1851)

Lord Palmerston (who became Prime Minister in 1855) reported the occasion to the British Ambassador in Paris:

...Mayne, the head of the police, told me he thought there were about thirty-four thousand in the glass building. The Queen, her husband, her eldest son and daughter, gave themselves in full confidence to this multitude, with no other guard than one of honour, and the accustomed supply of stick-handed constables, to assist the crowd in keeping order amongst themselves...

The royal party were received with continued acclamation as they passed through the parks and round the Exhibition House; and it was also very interesting to witness the cordial greeting given to the Duke of Wellington...

The building itself is far more worth seeing than anything in it, though many of its contents are worthy of admiration...

(Letter from Lord Palmerston to Lord Normanby (Ambassador in Paris); in E. Ashley, *Life and Correspondence of Lord Palmerston*, Bentley, 1879, vol. ii, p. 178)

The exhibits

Queen Victoria, a frequent visitor to the Exhibition, recorded in her journal:

Went to the machinery part, where we remained two hours, and which is excessively interesting and instructive... What used to be done by hand and used to take months doing is now accomplished in a few instants by the

The Machinery hall at the Great Exhibition

most beautiful machinery. We saw first the cotton machines from Old-ham . . . We saw hydraulic machines, pumps, filtering machines of all kinds, machines for purifying sugar – in fact, every conceivable invention. We likewise saw medals made by machinery which not more than fifteen years ago were made by hand, fifty million instead of one million can be supplied in a week now.
(In Eric de Maré, *The Year of the Great Exhibition*, The Folio Society, 1972)

Britain's leadership in industry over other countries was obvious from an examination of the exhibits. A French visitor noted:

While the foreign nave is filled with objects of art, properly speaking, the English is principally occupied by objects of utility.
(In de Maré, *The Year of the Great Exhibition*, 1972)

Part of the foreign exhibit at the Great Exhibition

Visiting the Great Exhibition

A visit to the Great Exhibition was thought of as an important social occasion.
Even so, many people had their doubts about the safety of such an unusual building, while others feared the possible outcome of gathering together such a huge
crowd. Lady Charlotte Guest recorded her impressions:

> *April 30th*
>   A large and pleasant party at Lady John Russell's. Everybody was talking
> of tomorrow's opening. Most people were going, but some few professed to
> treat it with contempt, and some had not thought it worth while to take
> season tickets, by which admission could be had. Some days before, a great
> deal had been said about the dangers attendant on the ceremony. Some
> affirmed that the whole edifice would tumble down, some that the noise of
> the cannons would shatter the glass, many that the crowd and rush at the
> doors would be intolerable, and not a few expected that riots and rebellions
> and conspiracies were suddenly to break out . . .
> (Earl of Bessborough, *The Diaries of Lady Charlotte Guest* (*1833–52*),
> 1950, Chapter XV, pp. 268–71)

To the Great Exhibition

Such fears were not justified, however. The Exhibition was tremendously popular, and people came from all over Britain to visit it. Cheap railway travel allowed many working people to make the journey of their lives to see the Exhibition in London. The *Illustrated London News* reported:

> Already the working classes in Manchester, Liverpool, Sheffield, Birmingham, the Potteries and the other great iron districts between Glasgow and Airdrie, as well as other places, have commenced laying by their weekly pence to form a fund for visiting London during the Great Exhibition of 1851. Were it not for cheap excursion trains this great source of amusement and instruction would have been unobtainable and the Exhibition would have lost one of its great attractions.
> (*Illustrated London News*, 21 September 1850)

People from all classes and occupations managed to visit the Exhibition:

> The classes who could afford to pay for their admission having had their

turn, from the holders of season tickets, and the more aristocratic and exclusive visitors who love elbow-room in their amusements, down to the five-shilling Saturday people, the half-crown Friday people, and the great bulk . . . in somewhat humbler circumstances, who congregate on the shilling days, the turn of those who are too poor to pay for such an amusement has come also . . . the doors of the Crystal Palace have been opened to many thousands of industrious, grateful, well-behaved, and admiring people, without cost to themselves . . . Clergymen and landed proprietors in remote rural districts have organised plans by which whole troops of agricultural labourers, with their wives and children, have been enabled to visit London once in their lives, and to see the marvels of art, skill, and industry congregated together in a building so novel in its construction, and so imposing in appearance . . . Manufacturers in the provincial towns . . . have not only given their workpeople a holiday to enable them to visit the Exhibition, but have in numerous instances paid the expenses both of the trip and of their admission . . . Public companies and schools have done likewise . . . We rejoice to see such examples of kind feeling. They tend to obliterate the jealousies, that, to a greater or less extent, exist between the rich and poor. (*Illustrated London News*, No. 479, (vol. xviii), Saturday 28 June 1851)

The Exhibition was a great success. Over six million people visited it, and it made a fine profit of £160 000 – a tremendous amount of money at that time. This was used to buy land on which was built the South Kensington Museums and Colleges.

The famous 'Crystal Palace' was closed to the public in October, 1851. It was then taken down and re-built at Sydenham, where it was re-opened in 1854 as a site for all sorts of exhibitions and entertainments. Unfortunately, it was destroyed by fire in November, 1936.

The Great Exhibition showed how Britain had changed between 1815 and 1851. Although the Industrial Revolution had begun in the late eighteenth century, in 1815, more people in Britain were still employed on the land than in industry. More people still lived in the countryside than in the towns and cities. Industrial development had progressed so fast, however, that after 1851, the opposite was true.

(Opposite) *Over London by rail (A railway passenger's view of London slums)*

QUESTIONS

1   State in your own words the purpose of holding an international exhibition, according to Prince Albert.

2   (a) Make a list of the goods on display at the Great Exhibition.
   (b) Compare the exhibits in the British and foreign sections. What difference do you notice, and what difference does this show between Britain and other countries in 1851?

3   (a) What different reasons did some people have for actually fearing the opening of the Great Exhibition?
   (b) What was the only measure taken to maintain order?

4   Find as many reasons as you can why it was possible for working people from all over Britain to visit London for the Exhibition.

5   What turning-point had been reached by Britain in the year 1851, as represented by the Great Exhibition?

ASSIGNMENT

Imagine you were visiting the Great Exhibition from your home area outside London. Describe your visit to a friend on your return, mentioning how you were able to afford the cost of the journey, your impressions of the 'Crystal Palace', the opening of the Exhibition, the people present, and the exhibits you saw.

Glossary

Agent Provacateur	A government spy who collected information on Radical activities. They often encouraged Radicals to break the law in order to arrest them.
Commissioner	A person appointed by the government to serve on a Royal Commission to investigate some matter of public concern, for example, working conditions in mines and factories, living conditions in the industrial towns, the working of the Poor Law.
Domestic industry	The manufacture of cloth by hand (both spinning and weaving) by villagers at home before the development of factory industry.
Enclosures	Hedged or fenced (therefore, enclosed) fields which replaced the old open fields of scattered strips of land in the later eighteenth and early nineteenth centuries.
Franchise	The right to vote in elections.
Freehold	The right to hold property for life.
Free Trade	A system by which countries try to increase trade between them by removing customs duties on imported goods. The phrase was first used by Adam Smith in his book *The Wealth of Nations* in 1776. Later, William Huskisson and then Robert Peel reduced and abolished duties so that Britain was more or less a Free Trade country by 1850.
Habeas Corpus Act	A law which prevents a person being kept in prison after arrest without a trial. It was suspended by the government in 1817 because of the Radical disturbances taking place then.
Hustings	A platform from which candidates for Parliament made speeches, and on which voters had to indicate the candidate of their choice.
Laissez-faire	A policy of non-interference by the government in the freedom of the individual, especially in matters of trade and industry.
Luddites	The name given to workers who smashed new machinery which was putting many of them out of work. They were named after 'Ned Ludd' and 'King Ludd' whose names appeared on letters protesting against the introduction of new machinery.

Pauper	A poor person who had to depend on poor relief because he or she could not earn a living.
Penal Code	The laws which lay down the punishments for different kinds of crimes.
Protection	The idea that customs duties should be charged on imported goods to make them more expensive than goods produced by manufacturers within a country. People might then buy cheaper goods produced by their own country, and encourage their own country's industries by doing so.
Radicals	People belonging to various groups who wanted far-reaching reforms, in particular, reform of Parliament, so that all adult males could vote at a General Election.
Suffrage	The right to vote. Also *Universal male suffrage*: a vote for every male adult.
Tories	Members of the Tory (later Conservative) Party, one of the two main political parties in Britain (the other party was the *Whigs*, see below). They supported the established order, including the monarch and the Church of England. Most of them regarded reform with suspicion.
Turnpike Trusts	Companies set up to build and repair roads. They paid for this by charging tolls for the use of the roads.
Whigs	Members of one of the two main political parties (the other being the Tory Party, see *Tories*, above.) They believed in reform of Parliament, Catholic emancipation and free trade.

Bibliography

*Denotes school textbook

GENERAL

*D. Richards and J.W. Hunt, *An Illustrated History of Modern Britain, 1783–1964*, Ch. 8, 9, 10, 11, Longman, 1965

*P.F. Speed, *Social Problems of the Industrial Revolution*, Wheaton, 1978

A. Briggs, *The Age of Improvement*, Longman, 1979

F. Engels, *The Condition of the Working Class in England*, 1844 (Panther, 1969)

E. Longford, *Wellington*, Vol. 2 *Pillar of State*, Weidenfeld & Nicolson, 1972

S. Smiles, *Self-Help*, London, 1859

A. Wood, *Nineteenth Century Britain*, Parts I, II, III, Longman, 1965

1 BRITAIN IN 1815

*P.F. Speed, *Social Problems of the Industrial Revolution*, Ch. 1, Wheaton, 1978

J.J. and A.J. Bagley, *The English Poor Law*, Macmillan, 1966

W. Cobbett, *Rural Rides*, Penguin English Library, 1967

R. Owen, *Observations on the Effect of the Manufacturing System*, 1815 (reprinted in G.D.H. Cole (ed) *A New View of Society and other writings by Robert Owen*, Dent (*Everyman's Library*), 1927)

2 UNREST AFTER 1815

S. Bamford, *Passages in the Life of a Radical*, Simpkin, 1844

G.D.H. Cole, *Life of William Cobbett*, Home & Van Thal, 1947

Memoirs of the Rt. Hon. the Earl of Liverpool, 1827

R.J. White, *Waterloo to Peterloo*, Heinemann, 1957

3 THE 'LIBERAL TORIES'

*P.F. Speed, *Police and Prisons*, Longman (*Then and There*) 1968

*P.F. Speed, *Social Problems of the Industrial Revolution*, Ch. 9, Wheaton, 1978

Memoir of Elizabeth Fry, London, 1847

J.J. Gurney, *Notes on a Visit made to some of the Prisons in Scotland and the North of England in company with Elizabeth Fry*, London, 1819.

J. Howard, *The State of the Prisons*, Dent (*Everyman's Library*), 1929

J. Kent, *Elizabeth Fry*, B.T. Batsford Ltd, 1962

Lord Mahon and E. Cardwell (eds), *Memoirs of Sir Robert Peel*, 1856–7.

4 PARLIAMENT
*J. Addy, *Parliamentary Elections and Reform, 1807–32*, Longman (*Then and There*), 1968
*J. Derry, *Parliamentary Reform*, Macmillan (*Sources of History*), 1966
*J.W. Hunt, *Reaction and Reform 1815–41*, Collins (*Britain in Modern Times*), 1972

5 WORKING IN FACTORIES AND MINES
*J. Addy, *A Coal and Iron Community in the Industrial Revolution*, Longman (*Then and There*), 1970
*E.G. Power, *A Textile Community in the Industrial Revolution*, Longman (*Then and There*), 1969
*P.F. Speed, *Social Problems of the Industrial Revolution*, Ch. 4, 5, Wheaton, 1978
 E. Hodder, *The Life and Work of the Seventh Earl of Shaftesbury*, London, 1887
 R. Owen, *Observations on the Effect of the Manufacturing System*, 1815 (See ch. 1 above)
 E.R. Pike, *Human Documents of the Industrial Revolution in Britain*, George Allen & Unwin, 1966

6 POVERTY AND HEALTH
*J.J. and A.J. Bagley, *The English Poor Law*, Macmillan, 1966
*P.F. Speed, *Social Problems of the Industrial Revolution*, Ch. 2, 3, 6, Wheaton, 1978
*R. Watson, *Edwin Chadwick: Poor Law and Public Health*, Longman (*Then and There*), 1969
 C. Dickens, *Oliver Twist*, London, 1838
 S.E. Finer, *The Life and Times of Edwin Chadwick*, Methuen, 1952
 E.R. Pike, *Human Documents of the Industrial Revolution in Britain*, George Allen & Unwin, 1966

7 WORKING CLASS MOVEMENTS
*R.D. Lobban, *The Trade Unions – A Short History*, Macmillan (*Sources of History*), 1969
*K.H. Randell, *Politics and People*, Collins (*New Advanced History*), 1972
*P. Searby, *The Chartists*, Longman (*Then and There*), 1967
*P.F. Speed, *Social Problems of the Industrial Revolution*, Ch. 8, Wheaton, 1978
*C. Thorne, *Chartism*, Macmillan (*Sources of History*), 1966
 G.D.H. Cole, *Chartist Portraits*, Macmillan, 1964
 H. Pelling, *A History of British Trade Unionism*, Macmillan, 1976

8 PEEL, FREE TRADE AND THE CORN LAW
Cobden's Speeches, 1870
The Devon Report: Digest of Evidence on Occupation of Land in Ireland, 1847
Lord Mahon and E. Cardwell (eds), *Memoirs of Sir Robert Peel*, 1856–7
D. Read, *Cobden and Bright: A Victorian Political Partnership*, Edward Arnold, 1967
A. Somerville, *The Whistler at the Plough*, 1852
C. Woodham-Smith, *The Great Hunger*, Hamish Hamilton, 1962

9 TRANSPORT IMPROVEMENTS

*M. Greenwood, *The Railway Revolution, 1825–45*, Longman (*Then and There*), 1955
*M. Greenwood, *Roads and Canals in the Eighteenth Century*, Longman (*Then and There*) 1953
*R.R. Sellman, *Brindley and Telford*, Methuen (*Brief Lives*), 1971
*R.R. Sellman, *George and Robert Stephenson*, Methuen (*Brief Lives*), 1971
*R.R. Sellman, *Isambard Kingdom Brunel*, Methuen (*Brief Lives*), 1971
*L.E. Snellgrove, *From 'Rocket' to Railcar*, Longman, 1963
 T. Coleman, *The Railway Navvies*, Pelican, 1968
 M. Robbins, *The Railway Age*, Penguin, 1965

10 BRITAIN IN 1851

*J.R.C. Yglesias, *London Life and the Great Exhibition*, Longman (*Then and There*), 1970
 The Great Exhibition, 1851: A Commemorative Album, H.M.S.O., 1964

Index